GENESIS to REVELATION

A Comprehensive Verse-by-Verse Exploration of the Bible

ROMANS
ROBERT JEWETT

LEADER GUIDE

GENESIS to REVELATION

A Comprehensive Verse-by-Verse Exploration of the Bible

ROMANS
ROBERT JEWETT

LEADER GUIDE

GENESIS TO REVELATION SERIES: **ROMANS**
LEADER GUIDE

ABINGDON PRESS
Nashville
Copyright © 1986, 1987 by Graded Press.
Revised Edition Copyright © 1997 by Abingdon Press.
Updated and Revised Edition Copyright © 2018 by Abingdon Press
All rights reserved.

ISBN 9781501855146

Manufactured in the United States of America
18 19 20 21 22 23 24 25 26 27—10 9 8 7 6 5 4 3 2 1

HOW TO TEACH GENESIS TO REVELATION

Unique Features of This Bible Study

In Genesis to Revelation, you and your class will study the Bible in three steps. Each step provides a different level of understanding of the Scripture. We call these steps Dimension One, Dimension Two, and Dimension Three.

Dimension One concerns what the Bible actually says. You do not interpret the Scripture at this point; you merely take account of what it says. Your main goal for this dimension is to get the content of the passage clear in your mind. What does the Bible say?

Dimension One is in workbook form. The members of the class will write the answers to questions about the passage in the space provided in the participant book. All the questions in Dimension One can be answered by reading the Bible itself. Be sure the class finishes Dimension One before going on to Dimensions Two and Three.

Dimension Two concerns information that will shed light on the Scripture under consideration. Dimension Two will answer such questions as

- What are the original meanings of some of the words used in the passage?

- What is the original background of the passage?

- Why was the passage most likely written?

- What are the relationships between the persons mentioned in the passage?

- What geographical and cultural factors affect the meaning of the passage?

The question for Dimension Two is, What information do we need in order to understand the meaning of the passage? In Dimension One the class members will discover what the Bible says. In Dimension Two they will discover what the Bible means.

Dimension Three focuses on interpreting the Scripture and applying it to life situations. The questions here are

- What is the meaning of the passage for my life?

- What response does the passage require of me as a Christian?

- What response does this passage require of us as a group?

Dimension Three questions have no easy answers. The task of applying the Scripture to life situations is up to you and the class.

Aside from the three-dimensional approach, another unique feature of this study is the organization of the series as a whole. Classes that choose to study the Genesis to Revelation Series will be able to study all the books of the Bible in their biblical order. This method will give the class continuity that is not present in most other Bible studies. The class will read and study virtually every verse of the Bible, from Genesis straight through to Revelation.

Weekly Preparation

Begin planning for each session early in the week. Read the passage that the lesson covers, and write the answers to Dimension One questions in the participant book. Then read Dimensions Two and Three in the participant book. Make a note of any questions or comments you have. Finally, study the material in the leader guide carefully. Decide how you want to organize your class session.

Organizing the Class Session

Since Genesis to Revelation involves three steps in studying the Scripture, you will want to organize your class sessions around these three dimensions. Each lesson in the participant book and this leader guide consists of three parts.

The first part of each lesson in the leader guide is the same as the Dimension One section in the participant book, except that the leader guide includes the answers to Dimension One questions. These questions and answers are taken from the New International Version of the Bible.

You might use Dimension One in several ways:

1. Ask the group members to read the Scripture and to write the answers to all the Dimension One questions before coming to class. This method will require that the class covenant to spend the necessary amount of study time outside of class. When the class session begins, read through the Dimension One questions, asking for responses from the group members. If anyone needs help with any of the answers, look at the biblical reference together.

2. Or, if you have enough class time, you might spend the first part of the session working through the Dimension One questions together as a group. Locate the Scripture references, ask the questions one at a time, and invite the class members to find the answers and to read them aloud. Then allow enough time for them to write the answers in the participant book.

3. Or, take some time at the beginning of the class session for group members to work individually. Have them read the Dimension One questions and the Scripture references and then write their answers to the questions in the spaces provided in the participant book. Discuss together any questions or answers in Dimension One that do not seem clear. This approach may take longer than the others, but it provides a good change of pace from time to time.

You do not have to organize your class sessions the same way every week. Ask the class members what they prefer. Experiment! You may find ways to study the Dimension One material other than the ones listed above.

The second part of each lesson in this leader guide corresponds to the second part of the participant book lessons. The Dimension Two section of the participant book provides background information to help the participants understand the Scripture. Become familiar with the information in the participant book.

Dimension Two of this leader guide contains additional information on the passage. The leader guide goes into more depth with some parts of the passage than the participant book does. You will want to share this information with the group in whatever way seems appropriate. For example, if someone raises a question about a particular verse, share any additional background information from the leader guide.

You might raise a simple question such as, What words or phrases gave you trouble in understanding the passage? or, Having grasped the content of the passage, what questions remain in your mind? Encourage the group members to share confusing points, troublesome words or phrases, or lingering questions. Write these problems on a posterboard or markerboard. This list of concerns will form the outline for the second portion of the session.

These concerns may also stimulate some research on the part of the group members. If your study group is large enough, divide the class into three groups. Then divide the passage for the following week into three parts. Assign a portion of the passage to each group. Using Bible commentaries and Bible dictionaries, direct each group to discover as much as it can about this portion of the passage before the class meets again. Each group will then report its findings during the class session.

The third part of each lesson in this leader guide relates to Dimension Three in the participant book. This section helps class members discover how to apply the Scripture to their own lives. Here you will find one or more interpretations of the passage—whether traditional, historical, or contemporary. Use these interpretations when appropriate to illumine the passage for the group members.

Dimension Three in the participant book points out some of the issues in the passage that are relevant to our lives. For each of these issues, the participant book raises questions to help the participants assess the meaning of the Scripture for their lives. The information in Dimension Three of the leader guide is designed to help you lead the class in discussing these issues. Usually, you will find a more in-depth discussion of portions of the Scripture.

The discussion in the leader guide will give you a better perspective on the Scripture and its interpretation before you begin to assess its meaning for today. You will probably want to share this Dimension Three information with the class to open the discussion. For each life situation, the leader guide contains suggestions on facilitating the class discussion. You, as the leader, are responsible for group discussions of Dimension Three issues.

Assembling Your Materials

You will need at least three items to prepare for and conduct each class session:

- A leader guide

- A participant book

- A Bible—you may use any translation or several; the answers in this leader guide are taken from the New International Version.

One advantage of the Genesis to Revelation Series is that the study is self-contained. That is, all you need to lead this Bible study is provided for you in the participant books and leader guides. Occasionally, or perhaps on a regular basis, you might want to consult other sources for additional information.

HOW TO LEAD A DISCUSSION

The Teacher as Discussion Leader

As the leader of this series or a part of this series, one of your main responsibilities during each class period will be to lead the class discussion. Some leaders are apprehensive about leading a discussion. In many ways, it is easier to lecture to the class. But remember that the class members will surely benefit more from the class sessions when they actively participate in a discussion of the material.

Leading a discussion is a skill that any teacher can master with practice. And keep in mind—especially if your class is not used to discussion—that the members of your group will also be learning through practice. The following are some pointers on how to lead interesting and thought-provoking discussions in the study group.

Preparing for a Discussion—Where Do I Start?

1. Focus on the subject that will be discussed and on the goal you want to achieve through that discussion.

2. Prepare by collecting information and data that you will need; jot down these ideas, facts, and questions so that you will have them when you need them.

3. Begin organizing your ideas; stop often to review your work. Keep in mind the climate within the group—attitudes, feelings, eagerness to participate and learn.

4. Consider possible alternative group procedures. Be prepared for the unexpected.

5. Having reached your goal, think through several ways to bring the discussion to a close.

As the leader, do not feel that your responsibility is to give a full account or report of the assigned material. This practice promotes dependency. Instead, through stimulating questions and discussion, the participants will read the material—not because you tell them to but because they want to read and prepare.

How Do I Establish a Climate for Learning?

The leader's readiness and preparation quickly establish a climate in which the group can proceed and its members learn and grow. The anxiety and fear of an unprepared leader are contagious but so are the positive vibrations coming from a leader who is prepared to move into a learning enterprise.

An attitude of shared ownership is also basic. Group members need to perceive themselves as part of the learning experience. Persons establish ownership by working on goals, sharing concerns, and accepting major responsibility for learning.

Here are several ways the leader can foster a positive climate for learning and growth.

1. Readiness. A leader who is always fully prepared can promote, in turn, the group's readiness to learn.

2. Exploration. When the leader encourages group members to freely explore new ideas, persons will know they are in a group whose primary function is learning.

3. Exposure. A leader who is open, honest, and willing to reveal himself or herself to the group will encourage participants to discuss their feelings and opinions.

4. Confidentiality. A leader can create a climate for learning when he or she respects the confidentiality of group members and encourages the group members to respect one another's confidentiality.

5. Acceptance. When a leader shows a high degree of acceptance, participants can likewise accept one another honestly.

How Can I Deal With Conflict?

What if conflict or strong disagreement arises in your group? What do you do? Think about the effective and ineffective ways you have dealt with conflict in the past.

Group conflict may come from one of several sources. One common source of conflict involves personality clashes. Any group is almost certain to contain at least two persons whose personalities clash. If you break your class into smaller groups for discussion, be sure these persons are in separate groups.

Another common source of group conflict is subject matter. The Bible can be a very controversial subject. Remember the difference between discussion or disagreement and conflict. As a leader you will have to decide when to encourage discussion and when to discourage conflict that is destructive to the group process.

Group conflict may also come from a general atmosphere conducive to expression of ideas and opinions. Try to discourage persons in the group from being judgmental toward others and their ideas. Keep reminding the class that each person is entitled to his or her own opinions and that no one opinion is more valid than another.

How Much Should I Contribute to the Discussion?

Many leaders are unsure about how much they should contribute to the class discussions. Below are several pitfalls to avoid.

1. The leader should remain neutral on a question until the group has had adequate time to discuss it. At the proper time in the discussion the leader can offer his or her opinion. The leader can direct the questions to the group at large, rechanneling those questions that come to him or her.

    At times when the members need to grapple with a question or issue, the most untimely response a leader can make is answering the question. Do not fall into the trap of doing the group members' work for them. Let them struggle with the question.

    However, if the leader has asked the group members to reveal thoughts and feelings, then group members have the right to expect the same of the leader. A leader has no right to ask others to reveal something he or she is unwilling to reveal. A leader can reveal thoughts and feelings, but at the appropriate time.

    The refusal to respond immediately to a question often takes self-discipline. The leader has spent time thinking, reading, and preparing. Thus the leader usually does have a point of view, and waiting for others to respond calls for restraint.

2. Another pitfall is the leader's making a speech or extended comments in expressing an opinion or summarizing what has been said. For example, in an attempt to persuade others, a leader may speak, repeat, or strongly emphasize what someone says concerning a question.

3. Finally, the pitfall of believing the leader must know "the answers" to the questions is always apparent. The leader need not know all the answers. Many questions that should be raised are ultimate and unanswerable; other questions are open-ended; and still others have several answers.

GENESIS TO REVELATION SERIES
ROMANS Leader Guide

Table of Contents

About the Writer

Dr. Robert Jewett served as Senior Scholar of New Testament Interpretation at Garrett-Evangelical Theological Seminary.

I am obligated both to Greeks and non-Greeks, both to the wise and the foolish. That is why I am so eager to preach the gospel also to you who are in Rome (1:14-15).

PAUL INTRODUCES HIMSELF

Romans 1:1-15

DIMENSION ONE: WHAT DOES THE BIBLE SAY?

Answer these questions by reading Romans 1:1-15

1. Identify the three expressions of Paul's self-identity in verses 1 and 5.

    In verse 1, Paul refers to himself as "a servant of Christ Jesus" and "called to be an apostle and set apart for the gospel of God." In verse 5, Paul says he has "received grace and apostleship to call all the Gentiles to the obedience that comes from faith."

2. Locate the description of the audience of the letter, the so-called "address" (1:7)

    Paul addresses his letter "to all in Rome who are loved by God and called to be his holy people."

3. Read the opening verses of the other Pauline letters (First and Second Corinthians, Galatians, Ephesians, Philippians, Colossians, First and Second Thessalonians, First and Second Timothy, Titus). Which openings contain a reference to the "gospel of God" promised through Scripture (1:1-2) or the creed concerning Jesus (1:3-4)?

    Of 1 Corinthians 1:1-3, 2 Corinthians 1:1-2, Galatians 1:1-5, Ephesians 1:1-2, Philippians 1:1-2, Colossians 1:1-2, 1 Thessalonians 1:1, 2 Thessalonians 1:1-2, 1 Timothy 1:1-2, 2 Timothy 1:1-2, and Titus 1:1-4, only Titus contains something similar to these references in Romans.

4. What does Paul mention as the content of his prayers in the "thanksgiving section"? (1:8-12)
   Paul reveals that he gives thanks for the faith of the Romans (1:8) and prays that he may visit them (1:10-11).

5. In the "narration section" (1:13-15) Paul explains both his motivation in visiting Rome and the reason he has not visited earlier. Identify both points.
   Paul's motivation is to "preach the gospel" (1:15) because he is "obligated" (1:14) to all the Gentiles. His earlier plans to visit Rome "have been prevented" (1:13).

DIMENSION TWO: WHAT DOES THE BIBLE MEAN?

The Problem of Teaching Romans

Romans is one of the most difficult books in the New Testament to teach, for several reasons. It does not fit the model of the other Pauline letters, which makes Romans hard to understand. For example, when people interpret Romans on the model of the Corinthian letters, they look at Romans as offering theological advice to a congregation that knows and respects Paul. This interpretation is obviously difficult because Paul did not found the church at Rome. Sometimes people interpret Romans on the model of Paul's letter to the Galatians, which is a defense of the gospel. When Romans is viewed this way, it is seen as a polemical letter, defending the true faith. The consequence of this view is that a particular approach to Romans, shaped perhaps by the Protestant or perhaps by the Roman Catholic tradition, is assumed to be the standard by which all other forms of the faith are being criticized by the Book of Romans. The crucial thrust of Romans as a document of early Christian pluralism is lost when the letter is approached in this way.

Many students of Romans, aware of the unique quality of the letter, understand it to be something of a theological treatise. They view Romans as a statement of pure doctrine, unrelated to any congregational situation. Since Paul had not been to Rome before writing the letter, people holding this view assume that Paul is summarizing his general teachings in a way that he thinks might be useful to the congregation. When this approach is taken, the missionary goal that Paul reveals in writing the letter is overlooked.

The peculiar abstraction of Romans also presents a barrier to understanding. That is, Romans is a formal writing with a large number of theological terms. These terms were each understandable in their original setting, but we easily become bogged down in a line-by-line and word-for-word debate on Romans. The problem of abstraction will prove particularly difficult for people in your group who think more concretely, who enjoy pictures and parables, and who lack formal philosophical or theological training.

The approach I suggest is to place Romans in a vivid historical situation and to relate this situation to each section of the letter. The basic purpose of Romans was to gain support from the Roman house churches for Paul's mission to Spain. To achieve this purpose, Paul had to deal with the conflicts between the branches of the house churches in Rome. When these house churches are unified in purpose, free of conflict, and in harmony, then Paul can seek their support for organizing his proposed mission to a difficult portion of the Roman Empire, Spain. Keeping this concrete situation in mind may provide a lively accessibility to this complex letter.

The Structure of the Passage

The questions in Dimension One aim to make participants aware of the structure of Paul's introduction. When they compare the letter opening in Romans with the openings of other Pauline letters, the differences are going to become apparent. A grasp of these differences will help participants understand the unique purpose of Romans. You may want to write an outline of a typical letter opening on a whiteboard or on a large piece of paper. Your outline might look like this:

Sender—"Paul, a servant of Christ Jesus"

Recipient—"to all in Rome who are loved by God"

Greeting—"grace and peace to you"

This basic letter opening sometimes has slight expansions, but in no other letter are the expansions as large as in Romans.

Verses 1-7 reveal that Paul is introducing himself with considerable care to demonstrate the orthodoxy of his gospel and the authenticity of his apostolic calling. You will note that the expansions in the letter opening are in sections 1 and 2. Themes of "apostle" and "gospel of God" announced in verse 1 are developed in reverse order before Paul gets to the address of the letter. Part of this expansion involves the citation of an early Christian creed in verses 3-4. Quite likely, this creed is a composite of the viewpoints of conservative and liberal Christians in Rome; and many commentators feel that the creed was actually being used in the Roman house churches.

Verses 8-12 make up the "thanksgiving" section in the introduction to Romans. In most instances the thanksgiving of a Pauline letter announces the major themes of the letter and reveals Paul's purpose in writing. Note that the thanksgiving proper is only in verse 8 but that the themes of prayer and of the relationship between the believers before God continues. The thing that Paul stresses in this section is that he has long prayed to be able to travel to Rome in order to preach the gospel there. This reveals the most important reason why Paul is addressing this letter to a church that he does not know: He wishes to visit them in order to preach the gospel and to involve them in fulfilling the missional thrust of their faith that has already been "reported all over the world."

The final section in this lesson is the narration in verses 13-15. These verses explain the background of Paul's intended visit to Rome, stressing that his plans have repeatedly been frustrated. Paul's desire to preach in Rome is related in verse 14 to his feeling of obligation to preach the gospel to all persons everywhere. In verse 15 the narration ends on the theme of Paul's eagerness to preach the gospel to the Christians in Rome.

The unique structure and content of this introduction, thanksgiving, and narration serve to lead the congregation into Paul's letter and more importantly into the project for which he hopes to gain their cooperation, the mission to Spain. The content of this introduction is matched to some degree by the conclusion of the letter in Romans 15 and 16. Although we will not be dealing with these chapters until the next lesson, a knowledge of their content is essential for understanding Romans 1:1-15.

In Romans 15, Paul explicitly mentions the plan to carry his mission to Spain (15:24, 28). He also discusses some of the factors that have hindered his earlier arrival in Rome, including the difficulties in connection with the Jerusalem offering. Paul's great skill as a writer is shown as he lightly introduces these themes in Romans 1 and lays out his formal argument before returning to the precise details in Romans 15, details that might have alienated the congregation without the proper background.

Romans 1:1. The word *servant* in verse 1 is often translated "slave," which is sometimes felt to be far too humble for the high apostolic office that Paul claims in verses 1-5. Actually, the term *slave* had a formal bureaucratic meaning for the Roman audience. The Roman bureaucracy that was rapidly developing at the time Paul wrote this letter was made up of highly trained and highly paid slaves of Caesar. These persons were preferred in the imperial offices because they were loyal to the emperor alone, hoping for their freedom after some years of loyal service. Many of the slaves serving in the imperial bureaucracy became fabulously rich because of their handling of imperial finances. Also, during the time Paul wrote, the expression "slave of Caesar" was often used for imperial ambassadors or representatives of various kinds. Such persons carried the majesty and power of the emperor with them as they represented him in foreign courts.

The connotation that is most likely for 1:1 is, "Paul, an *ambassador* of Christ Jesus." In this way he was introduced to the Roman congregation with a term that had an official sound. Paul introduces himself as a representative of Christ, the one who advocates his gospel and promotes the cause of his Kingdom. The term *apostle* simply means a messenger or a person sent to deliver a specific message and/or to perform a specific mission. The term was often used in secular settings for a representative sent off on an errand by someone else. In this instance Paul qualifies the term *apostle* by the expression *called*, referring to his election to missionary activity at the time of his conversion.

Romans 1:3-4. The early Christian creed cited in verses 3 and 4 begins after the word *Son*. A literal translation is as follows:

Born from David's seed according to the flesh, appointed Son of God in power according to the spirit of holiness, through the resurrection of the dead.

This confession likely originated in Jewish-Christian circles, with a stress on the messianic line from David and the appointment as Son of God through the Resurrection. This early creed is very close to some of the creeds found in the Book of Acts, stressing the seed of David and the adoption of Jesus as the Son of God on the basis of the Resurrection.

Apparently the liberal Hellenistic Christians had edited this creed. They would have wished to downplay the nationalistic component of David's seed and to stress the power of the Spirit. They inserted the lines "as to his earthly life" and "through the Spirit" in order to affirm that the business of David's seed was only on a fleshly and therefore human level, whereas the appointment of Jesus as the Son of God was by direct divine intervention, according to the Spirit. This addition made the creed universal, opening it up to people who were not of Jewish background and who were not loyal to the messianic hope of Israel.

Paul probably made the final change to the creed, adding the words "of holiness" to the phrase "through the Spirit." This revised phrase counters the tendency of those persons in the early church who liked to think in dualistic terms, opposing "flesh" to "spirit." As we know from the Corinthian letters in particular, the liberals who were most conscious of being in the Spirit tended at times to believe that they were superior to "fleshly" rules such as the Ten Commandments. The problem of libertinism, of believing that one is above the law, is countered at a number of other points in Romans, which indicates that this was something of a problem in the Roman house churches. By emphasizing holiness, Paul makes clear that the spirit of a new era is consistent with ethical responsibility.

Romans 1:5. In verse 5, Paul shifts from the first person singular to the first person plural: "*We received grace and apostleship.*" Paul often speaks of himself in the first person plural, and in many instances he is referring to himself and his coworkers. Paul had a shared sense of missionary obligation. He wrote most of his letters in collaboration with his missionary colleagues. Since the Romans did not know Paul and his missionary team, it was inappropriate in this instance to mention them in the opening chapter. But it is worth observing that in Romans 16, Paul mentions greetings from Timothy and a number of other close colleagues.

Romans 1:6-7. You and the group members may notice a conspicuous omission in verse 7. Unlike the other letters addressed to Pauline congregations, this opening does not refer to a "church." This omission is perhaps due to the fact that only one of the five house churches mentioned in Romans 16 referred to itself as "church." Keep in mind that Romans was written at a time before a standard set of terms had come into use for early Christians. Each congregation probably called itself something different, especially in a place where the church was as decentralized as it was in Rome.

The suggestion in the participant book is that Paul uses two typical names for church members in verses 6 and 7. He refers to one group as "called to belong to Jesus Christ," probably used for liberals and Gentile Christians. The title "called to be his holy people" probably is used for conservatives and Jewish Christians. Paul is being sensitive to the fact that not everyone has a consciousness of being in a "church." Therefore I think it is significant that the title of church membership that he places between the first and third titles is unique to Romans, namely, "all . . . who are loved by God." Paul wishes to stress that all Christians in Rome, whether conservative or liberal, whether Jewish Christian or Gentile Christian, are equal in God's love.

Romans 1:8-12. The stress on inclusivity is carried on in verse 8 where Paul gives thanks "for all of you" in his prayers. Sensitivity to congregational feelings is also shown in verses 11 and 12. In verse 11, Paul boldly states that he wishes to impart a "spiritual gift" or blessing, which might have been taken to imply that Paul did not feel that the congregation had spiritual power and fell short in some way. Paul immediately adds the tactful words in verse 12 to make clear that he expects to learn as much as he teaches when he comes to Rome.

Romans 1:13. In verse 13, where Paul describes the events behind his planned visit, he refers to the hindrances that have prevented his earlier arrival. Read 2 Corinthians 11:24-28 for an example of the kind of hindrances Paul had in mind. This section of the Corinthian correspondence was probably written not too long before Paul wrote Romans. By correlating the details of 2 Corinthians 8 and 9 with the indications of the problem in collecting the Jerusalem offering, we can see that the discord in Corinth set Paul's plan back for at least a year. Also, he was imprisoned more than once during this time. Acts 20:1-3 indicates other reasons for delays, namely, the hostility of Jewish zealots against Paul who were behind some of Paul's other imprisonments and troubles as well. His hope, as shown in

Romans 15, had been to complete his work in the eastern mission field, deliver the offering, and arrive in Rome in order to get to Spain as quickly as possible. Paul's plans were delayed at least two and perhaps three years by the various forms of adversity that he experienced in his mission work.

Romans 1:14-15. In verse 14 "the wise and the foolish" probably relates to educational level. One might think of "the wise" as the highly educated and "the foolish" as working-class people and slaves who did not have the benefit of higher education.

Paul stresses he is obligated to both sides of this stereotype. Paul makes it clear, therefore, that in the church, stereotypes like this are of no effect any longer. Paul implies in verse 15 that all these groups (Greeks and non-Greeks, wise and foolish) are represented in Rome and that his broad sense of responsibility is what leads him to include everyone.

DIMENSION THREE:
WHAT DOES THE BIBLE MEAN TO ME?

In light of the problem of abstraction in dealing with Romans discussed earlier, I suggest that you spend a fair amount of time in the opening session dealing with the question of what the Roman church situation means to us today.

The Unique Circumstances of a Congregation

In connection with the unique history of the Roman house churches, marked by adversity and conflict, reflect on the parallels with the experience of your local congregation. Tensions between conservatives and liberals may be relevant for your particular situation. The experience of serious disruption in the life of the congregation caused by external circumstances may be appropriate in case of fire, natural disasters, and so on. The growing divide among people of different political persuasions is also played out in local churches. The competition among church leaders and groups loyal to particular leaders is also widely experienced in the modern church. The situation in Rome of having too many leaders of the congregation in competition for spaces might be similar to a situation of a denomination having too many ministerial members for the number of churches available. The conflicts caused by changes in liturgy, hymns, and location of worship services may parallel experiences your congregation has had in the past. If your congregation is trying to find its way in the midst of internal conflict, addressing it may be helpful, though with Paul's intentional and careful tact.

The point of thinking through these connections is to see the vivid parallels between modern church situations and the circumstances to which Romans was addressed. Only by making this imaginative leap can the abstract quality of the argument of Romans be overcome and the relevance of its argument perceived.

In connection with thinking about the unique circumstances of an individual congregation, it would be worth pointing out that Romans is addressed in a peculiar way to a peculiar congregation. In none of Paul's other letters does he address a congregation in just this manner. So each modern congregation also needs to be addressed by the gospel in unique and distinctive ways, reflecting their unique circumstances.

The task of a study of Romans, therefore, is to think through the connections between the ancient situation and the modern situation, to adapt Paul's argument to our different circumstances today for our particular congregation. No one interpretation of Romans is ever going to be universally relevant. Each congregation must discover the meaning of Romans for itself; each study group must follow the same process of discovery.

What parallels do you see locally with the situation of the church in Rome? In what ways does your congregation work for internal unity and for community solidarity in the name of Christ?

Mutual Encouragement and Exhortation

We need tact and mutual respect when dealing with Romans. Part of this need is caused by the fact that the dogmatic tradition of past interpreters leads to preset formulas that tend to be argued in hostile manners by some persons. The abstraction of the argument of Romans leads certain people with an affinity to this kind of thinking to dominate others whose thought is more concrete and detailed. The elements of tact that are visible in the opening of Romans provide good models for both the leader of a Romans study and the participants. In particular we need to live up to the principle of 1:12, involving mutual encouragement and exhortation, rather than the leader laying down the truth for everyone else. Consistent with the content of this letter, you need to encourage mutuality, respect, and encouragement for the contributions of each member.

Inclusiveness

Paul's stress on inclusiveness also offers a significant resource for structuring a study of Romans. The diversity in theological outlook, background, and history of the members of a typical study group need to be brought to the fore in order to show the parallels to the diversity of the Roman house churches. The formulas that Paul uses (for example, 1:14) might well be adapted to the situation in your group. The Greeks might be like those who speak a particular form of English, whereas the non-Greeks might be those for whom English is a second language. The wise might be those with university degrees, and the foolish might be those with a grammar-school education. As we all know, some of the most intelligent persons in a group are often the ones with the least formal education. The diversity in educational level and cultural background in the group can be used to make plain the parallels between the Roman church situation and the situation in your local congregation.

The effort on Paul's part to include everyone, his frequent use of the word *all*, is a worthy model for your group. Paul's inclusiveness is particularly clear in the confession in verses 3-4. He does not take sides as to which version of the creed is most appropriate. He makes a small correction and simply cites the creed, thus making legitimate the viewpoint of both conservatives and liberals. Paul's effort is to unite, not to promote a single "right view." This strategy is appropriate for your group.

You need to honor the theological perspective and religious experience of each member in the group, to seek for common ground, and to encourage mutual respect in the midst of divergent opinions and interpretations.. Romans is written to a series of house churches who are going to remain in disagreement. The whole question is whether they can be sufficiently united in the gospel to agree on a common mission. That is the agenda, not only of the Roman house churches, but for the modern church as well.

I glory in Christ Jesus in my service to God (15:17).

PAUL'S PURPOSE AND SITUATION

Romans 15:14–16:2

DIMENSION ONE: WHAT DOES THE BIBLE SAY?

Answer these questions by reading Romans 15:14–16:2

1. What are the references to the Spanish mission in this passage? (15:24, 28)

   Paul writes, "I plan to do so when I go to Spain"; and, "I will go to Spain and visit you on the way."

2. What details in our previous lesson on Romans 1:1-15 are similar to Romans 15:14, where Paul compliments the Romans for being "full of goodness, filled with knowledge and competent to instruct one another"?

   In 1:8, Paul refers to the Romans' faith as being "reported all over the world"; and in 1:12, he expresses the hope to "be mutually encouraged by each other's faith," which implies they are able to instruct others.

3. What is the geographic scope of Paul's previous mission? (15:19)

   The scope of Paul's earlier mission is from Jerusalem to Illyricum.

4. How long does Paul plan to spend in Rome? (15:24)

   Paul plans to stay in Rome "for a while."

5. Does Paul plan to deliver the Jerusalem offering before or after he arrives in Rome? (15:25, 28)

   Paul plans to visit Rome after delivering the offering.

6. What does Paul request that the Romans do for Phoebe? (16:2)

Paul asks the Romans "to receive her in the Lord . . . and to give her any help she may need from you."

DIMENSION TWO:
WHAT DOES THE BIBLE MEAN?

Our motivation for moving to the end of Romans in this lesson is to come to terms with the historical situation behind this letter. The details concerning Paul's situation and his motivation for writing are found in the opening and closing sections, so this is where we must begin.

These sections of Romans are likely to be least understood and much less frequently read. Certainly, this material traditionally has not figured largely in the commentaries on Paul's letter to the Romans. But if we wish to overcome the dogmatic bias of our interpretive tradition—of viewing Romans as an abstract doctrinal treatise—it is essential that we take Paul's situation and motivation into account as we begin.

You need to understand the dramatic situation in which Paul's letter is actually placed. As we can see in 15:14–16:27, Paul is poised on the verge of several of his most daring and significant missionary enterprises. He is closing out the eastern mission field and is laying plans to complete the circuit of the Mediterranean world, moving toward Spain. Also, Paul is now ready to deliver the Gentile offering, which he hopes will unite the Gentile Christian and Jewish Christian wings of the church, thus preparing the way for the final mission.

Tragically, Paul ended up in Rome not as a free missionary but rather as a prisoner. The very process of carrying through this elaborate missionary scheme probably cost him his life. The political and personal aspects of Paul's situation at the time of writing this letter give the dramatic stage on which the letter should be interpreted.

Romans 15:14-19a. If we want to understand Paul's self-image, the second half of Romans 15 is the best place to look. Far from describing himself as a theologian, an abstract thinker, or a writer, Paul presents himself as a missionary to the Gentiles. The language he uses has often appeared puzzling. He speaks of himself in 15:16 as "a minister of Christ Jesus to the Gentiles. He gave me the priestly duty of proclaiming the gospel of God." Nowhere else in the Pauline letters do we have this kind of priestly wording used in Paul's self-description. This unusual description has led scholars to develop elaborate theories concerning Paul's understanding of himself.

The tendency of such theories, however, is to place Paul in the context of priestly institutions of established churches. This view overlooks the revolutionary, end-time horizon of his mission. It also leads to a misunderstanding of Paul's view of Christian ethics and of his view of the relation between Christians and Jews, if we conclude from this section that Paul advocates that a true Christian cult should replace a perverse Jewish cult.

The term *minister* in 15:16 is the same word used in 13:6 to describe governmental agents. This connotation of the word was widely used in the ancient world; it reflects the fact that priests and civil servants originally came from the same system and had interchangeable titles. We have something of that usage in modern language. In the terms of governmental officials in the British Commonwealth, the term *minister* is often used—Minister of Transportation, for example.

Minister therefore echoes the bureaucratic title that Paul used to describe himself in 1:1 as a "servant of Christ Jesus," meaning diplomat or agent of Jesus Christ. That this is the intended meaning of "minister of Christ Jesus" is further suggested by the phrase "to the Gentiles" that immediately follows it in 15:16. In the Roman world of the first century, this title would have sounded like the "Ambassador to the Parthians," or the like.

Paul understands himself here as the representative, the agent, of Jesus Christ to the Gentile world. Paul's task through the gospel is to restore the Gentile world to the holiness of the divine order, thereby completing the task of regenerating the world. For this reason he uses the phrase in verse 16, that "the Gentiles might become an offering acceptable to God, sanctified by the Holy Spirit." This language is reminiscent of the opening chapter of Romans, where Paul says, "we received grace and apostleship to call all the Gentiles to the obedience that comes from faith for his name's sake" (1:5).

A sweeping imperial vision is shown in the wording Paul uses to describe his vocation. Paul has the horizon of world mission in view; and he hopes for world conquest, not through force of arms, but through the power of the gospel. He understands himself in language that was directly parallel to that used by the Roman Empire. We can appropriately speak, therefore, of a fusion of the diplomatic, the bureaucratic, and the priestly viewpoints in this passage.

The crucial question for diplomacy, of course, is power. If the government one represents does not have sufficient power, then one's service is not likely to be effective. For this reason Paul is willing to say, in 15:17, "I glory in Christ Jesus in my service to God," which is elaborated in the following verses. The same Greek term is used here as in 3:27 for *boast*. Some translations, perhaps sensitive about the potential contradiction with Paul's rejection of arrogant "boasting" in 3:27, downplay this with the less offensive term *glory in*.

Paul concentrates here on the power that is in the gospel allowing him to lead "the Gentiles to obey God" (15:18). This theme of power surfaces in the thesis of Romans (1:16), a passage that we will be studying in Lesson 4. That the gospel "is the power of God that brings salvation to everyone who believes" is absolutely central for the argument of Romans. The means by which God will conquer the world, according to Paul, is not military or coercive force of any kind. The gospel changes people, leading them in a willing way under faith to work for the transformation of the world. When Paul returns to this theme in Romans 15, he draws together one of the most important emphases in his entire letter, the gospel as the power to transform the world.

In 15:18, Paul connects word and deed ("what I have said and done"). Unlike many modern theologians who tend to make the *word* of the gospel superior to *deeds*, Paul coordinates them. Ethics and theology are to be kept together. Both are inspired by the Spirit when properly carried out, and their integration is necessary for the gospel. The reference to "signs and wonders" in 15:19 refers to the miracles, healings, and spiritual transformations of early Christian missions. Unlike modern theologians and ministers, Paul does not separate the theological content of the gospel from "signs and wonders." Both reveal "the power of the Spirit" (15:19). Paul wants to make plain that this power, however, does not come from him personally. He is not a superman. The triumph of the gospel is due to what "Christ has accomplished through me" (15:18); Paul's success is entirely due to the "power of the Spirit" (15:19).

Romans 15:19b-23. Paul has a clear geographical horizon for his mission, as is shown in the wording of 15:19. We may think it odd to view the trip from Jerusalem as going "around" to Illyricum (which includes modern-day Serbia, Bosnia and Herzegovina, and Croatia) in a direction that obviously moves toward Rome and then on to Spain. We may also think it odd that Paul should refer to having "fully proclaimed the gospel," so that there was no more space for his activities in the East. We see here the peculiar world view of citizens of the Roman Empire whose conception of the world was shaped by the maps that were used by ancient travelers. Unlike our modern maps that give a projection with clear directions of north, south, east, and west, the maps of the Roman period were strip maps that showed the road network impressed into horizontal strips with directions given only on the basis of right or left. When one comes to a junction, one takes either the right turn or the left turn.

These maps showed the roads radiating out from Rome in every direction, and those that Paul had traveled in Asia Minor had the Mediterranean marked at the bottom of the strip map and the Black Sea marked at the top.

Paul's sense of the movement of the early Christian mission, therefore, was shaped by the Mediterranean and was moving in the direction of Rome and beyond. Paul had carried his mission as far west as Illyricum. From this point the strip maps showed ship connections across the Adriatic to the Roman road networks. Additional maps showed the Roman road connections on toward Spain, perceived in a real sense as the end of the world.

When we take this ancient world into account, we can see that Paul perceived his mission as one grand thrust from Jerusalem toward the end of the known world, namely Spain.

Paul was conscious of having "often been hindered" in arriving at Rome and completing the circle of his intended mission (15:22). Paul did not define the hindrance at this point but gave hints of his extensive missionary activities in 15:20-21. He gave other hints of the hindrances he had experienced in his greetings to missionary colleagues in 16:4 and 7. Two of the leaders Paul names, Priscilla and Aquila, had saved Paul's life on one occasion, risking their own lives in the process. And Andronicus and Junia were fellow prisoners with Paul.

When we reconstruct all the difficulties Paul had faced in the two-year period prior to writing Romans, the "hindrance" becomes clear. Paul was probably imprisoned at least two times and had a narrow escape from a third imprisonment. He had to deal with problems in the congregations at Colossae, Philippi, Laodicea, and Corinth. Many of these troubles required Paul to travel, to write letters, or to send missionary colleagues. He also had to face several postponements of the plans for collecting and sending the Jerusalem offering, which had to be completed before Paul would be free to pursue the circle path toward Spain.

Romans 15:24-33. What was there about the Spanish mission that required the tactful and elaborate preparation of a letter to the Romans and the sending of Phoebe? If indeed the entire letter was directly related to this project, why was it necessary? Could Paul not have completed the circle of the Mediterranean world by going straight to Spain? And why not begin a mission in Spain as he had in Thessalonica or Corinth? Why not simply arrive, start off preaching in a synagogue, get a foothold, take up work with a colleague like Priscilla and Aquila, and begin the kind of self-supporting mission that he had organized in the centers of the East?

Several factors could be suggested in answer to these questions. First, in the ancient world "all roads led to Rome." It would literally have been very difficult for Paul to travel from Corinth (where he was), or even from Jerusalem (where he planned to depart), and arrive in Spain without passing through Rome. The travel routes of the entire Roman Empire radiated out from Rome in all directions.

A second, more significant, factor was that Paul's usual missionary strategy was to begin by visiting and preaching in the local synagogue. Only after conflicts arose in that synagogue would he establish a new Christian house church in someone's home, if he could find a patron. Early commentaries on Romans assumed that Jewish synagogues were established in Spain at the time Paul wrote Romans. But more recent studies indicate that Spain had neither large groups of Jewish settlers nor any synagogues during the first century. Jewish immigration to Spain did not begin until after the Jewish-Roman War of AD 66–70, more than a decade after Paul wrote Romans. Immigration was intensified after the Jewish revolt of AD 132–135. Doubtless early commentators on Romans had been led astray by outdated information on this issue, and the entire project of the Spanish mission and its strategy needs to be thought through again as a consequence.

The lack of a Jewish community in Spain would pose a serious barrier to Paul's mission. There would be no previous readiness to hear a message about an expected Messiah based on Jewish missionary preaching. Paul could not count on God-fearers or proselytes in the Spanish cities to create the cells of believing communities.

The lack of a Jewish community would also pose a significant economic problem to Paul. We know that the Jewish synagogues filled a social and economic as well as a religious function in the Greek and Roman cities. Travelers would use the small hostel attached to a typical synagogue when first arriving in a community. An easy network within the Jewish community in a city would thus be made available, and this would provide an avenue for employment opportunities. As a self-sustaining worker in the tent and leather business, Paul depended on such contacts to make his meager living. The problem of finding a "base of operations" would therefore be quite severe in Spain because of the lack of a Jewish population.

Another barrier to Christian mission in Spain related to the cultural environment: Spain had no Greek culture so far as recent studies have indicated. In fact, Latin, the official language of the western part of the Empire, was only used in the major urban centers. The rural population in most places continued to speak the obscure dialects of the original population before the Roman conquest. The linguistic barriers that Paul would face would therefore be quite severe. We know that he spoke Greek and Hebrew, but we have no indication that he had command of Latin. The Christian communities that had centered in the synagogues in Rome were also Greek speaking rather than Latin speaking, though several would have had resources for Latin within the congregation. Nevertheless, we do not know whether a tradition had already been established for proclaiming the gospel in Latin at the time Paul wrote. His missionary activity therefore would depend on translators.

An additional factor was that a series of Spanish revolts against Roman rule in the generation before Paul arrived led the imperial authorities to confiscate large amounts of private property. This property was placed in the hands of state authorities or of loyal citizens elsewhere in the Empire who could afford to pay for them. The populace was in many instances quite resistant to Roman rule. While resources from Rome would be absolutely crucial to getting a foothold in Spain, Paul could not put himself in a position of entering Spain as an agent of the Roman churches. This would have appeared far too imperialistic for the sensitive feelings of the Spaniards.

To mount an effective Spanish mission, therefore, required a wisely selected logistical base, the provision of formidable translation resources, and support from persons in Rome who were not identified in Spain as agents of the government. To provide these resources and to get the mission in Spain off on the right foot, Paul needed wise counsel and the cooperation of a wide range of resources within the Roman house churches, which at the time of his writing Romans were locked in conflict with one another. Paul desperately needed a peacemaker who could work out the arrangements for the Spanish mission before he arrived. This is where Phoebe comes into our story.

Romans 16:1-2. In Question 6 of Dimension One, you find the request that Paul makes for Phoebe in Romans 16:2. This might provide a take-off point for discussing the details concerning this remarkable and largely unheralded woman. Phoebe was probably named after a Greek goddess, which indicates to us that she could not have been of Jewish background. She is introduced to the Romans as "our sister," which indicates membership in the early Christian community. The terms *sister* and *brother* were often used in the early church to show membership. The word *our* carries the nuance of her belonging to Paul as well as to all other Christians. *Our* has a legitimizing function. Phoebe is not an outsider to Rome, in a sense; she belongs to the whole Christian community as "our sister."

Paul goes on to identify Phoebe as a "deacon of the church in Cenchreae." Our impression is that in the first generation of Christian leadership, each church had its own name for church leaders. Some called their leaders presbyters; others, bishops; others, deacons. Our impression, therefore, is that she is a leader of this particular congregation.

The most revealing title used for Phoebe, however, is the term translated in the participant book as "patroness." It might be wise to ask participants to check the various Bible translations they have at this point. Paul uses a technical term here that means the "protector" or the "patron," which had a clear legal and social connotation in the Greco-Roman world. Patrons and patronesses were upper-class figures who provided legal protection for their employees, slaves, friends, and dependents. The term that Paul uses here is associated with the Latin term *patrona*, which is closely related to the modern Italian term that is translated as "godfather" in popular American usage. We should think of Phoebe as a wealthy woman with a large estate who provides legal protection, employment, and leadership for the people around her.

Understanding Phoebe's social class helps us understand Paul's description of her activities in the Christian mission: "She has been the benefactor [patroness] of many people, including me" (16:2). This means that Phoebe had provided travel funds and support for a number of early

Christian missionaries and that Paul was dependent on her as well. When he asks the Roman Christians to "receive her in the Lord in a way worthy of his people," he is asking for them to roll out the red carpet for this prestigious and significant leader in the early Christian mission. And it is clear in the context that the help Phoebe requires is the task of her patronage.

Part of Phoebe's task would be to unify the Roman house churches by bringing Paul's letter to the churches, discussing its contents, and gaining assent to the plan to carry the mission to Spain. She would need to convince the house churches in Rome that Paul was a trustworthy partner for the Spanish mission. This task would be difficult, given Paul's involvement in so many controversial projects and conflicts. Conservative Jewish Christians would have known him as the radical Gentile missionary, the opponent of the Judaizer campaign. But the house churches close to the Roman government would be concerned over Paul's conflicts with provincial authorities, his several imprisonments and involvements at public disturbances. The potential damage that cooperation with a controversial troublemaker might cause for the images of their churches in Rome would cause them to be quite careful. Therefore, to gain their collective support for a project headed by Paul would not be easy.

Finally and most importantly, Phoebe's task would be to make the political contacts through Rome with potential supporters of a Pauline mission to Spain. This would involve providing a base of operations for Paul and his missionary colleagues, providing support for their travels and lodging, and providing translators capable of moving from Greek to Latin as well as to the Spanish dialects. Experienced advisors would be required in Rome to help find the right contacts in Spain and to use their influence to develop those contacts. Careful and wise preparation would have to be carried out ahead of time to make a Spanish mission feasible. A considerable amount of financial assistance would be required to replace the self-supporting missionary strategy that Paul had used, starting in the Jewish synagogues and other locations.

DIMENSION THREE:
WHAT DOES THE BIBLE MEAN TO ME?

Mutual Sharing and Solidarity

The rationale for stewardship that Paul provides in Romans is quite striking in its contrast with some modern approaches. Paul emphasizes mutual sharing and solidarity. His premise is that you cannot give before you have received and that you receive out of a sense of mutual indebtedness. This seems quite different from the modern approach of encouraging people to contribute out of either guilt or a sense of generosity. Also, Paul's sense that stewardship should provide a means of overcoming racial and cultural barriers is a provocative resource for the modern church.

In what ways do Paul's ideas of giving out of mutual indebtedness have a bearing on the church today? Even in a generosity model, giving can be seen as a flow of gifts from "greater to lesser" or from "superior to inferior." Does your (or your church's) model of stewardship provide any opportunity for reciprocity from recipients? Do you or the church expect or ask anything in return? If so, how is that expectation presented and in what attitude?

The Role of Women in the Church

The discovery of the crucial role of leadership by women in the Pauline mission movement is a striking one. Not only was Phoebe crucial for Paul's mission, a number of female missionary partners are recommended as reliable in 16:3-15, the material we shall study in our next lesson. One is struck by the role that could be played by an upper-class woman like Phoebe, whose business contacts and prestige would give her access to the wide range of Roman churches to achieve the delicate diplomatic task of unifying that church. Later developments in the Christian church also had a prominent role for women. One feature of such movements, however, is that in the second generation often the leadership role of women is crowded out by other considerations. At times of rapid expansion, however, women have played a very important role. The equality produced by the gospel calls forth the resources of both sexes in equal measure.

What might those "other considerations" be, and what is your assessment of their validity, at least today? The statements that seem to exclude the leadership of women in letters attributed to Paul, but not genuinely his, still hold power in some churches and denominations. Where would your congregation be without the leadership and support of women? In what ways does your congregation nurture growth and leadership training for any member who shows leadership gifts?

We who are strong ought to bear with the failings of the weak (15:1).

THE WEAK AND THE STRONG IN ROME

Romans 14:1–15:13; 16:3-27

DIMENSION ONE:
WHAT DOES THE BIBLE SAY?

Answer these questions by reading Romans 14:1–15:13; 16:3-27

1. Who is in the outsider position and needs to be welcomed? (14:1)
   Paul writes that "the one whose faith is weak" is to be welcomed.

2. Whom does Paul favor, the "weak" who consider "one day more sacred than another" and abstain "to the Lord" or the "strong" who do the opposite? (14:5-9)
   Paul's argument justifies each side as long as an individual member is "fully convinced in their own mind."

3. Since Paul's personal belief matches that of the "strong," who believe that "nothing is unclean in itself" (14:14), what approach does he advocate for others? (14:15, 23)
   Paul urges the "strong" to avoid imposing their views on the "weak." He urges the "weak" to remain true to their principles.

4. What does the example of Christ support? (15:1-6)
   The example of Christ in these verses supports acceptance and tolerance and promotes "the same attitude of mind . . . that Christ Jesus had."

5. How many times is the term *Gentiles* used in 15:8-12?
   Paul uses the term Gentiles twice in verse 9 and once each in verses 10, 11, and 12.

6. List the names of those whom Paul greets with a reference about either their experiences with him or their personal qualities. (16:3-15)

> *1. Priscilla (16:3); 2. Aquila (16:3); 3. Epenetus (16:5); 4. Mary (16:6); 5. Andronicus (16:7); 6. Junia (16:7); 7. Ampliatus (16:8); 8. Urbanus (16:9); 9. Stachys (16:9); 10. Apelles (16:10); 11. Tryphena (16:12); 12. Tryphosa (16:12a); 13. Persis (16:12b); 14. Rufus (16:13); 15. Rufus's mother (16:13).*

7. List the names of those whom Paul greets without any personal references to indicate that he has met or worked with them. (16:3-15)

> *1. The family of Aristobulus (16:10b); 2. Herodion (16:11); 3. the family of Narcissus (16:11b); 4. Asyncritus (16:14); 5. Phlegon (16:14); 6. Hermes (16:14); 7. Patrobas (16:14); 8. Hermas (16:14); 9. Philologus (16:15); 10. Julia (16:15); 11. Nereus (16:15); 12. Nereus's sister (16:15); 13. Olympas (16:15).*

8. List the pairs of names that are linked together and/or give some other indication of being family members. (16:3-15)

> *1. Priscilla and Aquila (16:3), a married couple; 2. Andronicus and Junia (16:7), probably a married couple; 3. Tryphena and Tryphosa (16:12), probably sisters, possibly twins; 4. Rufus and his mother (16:13); 5. Nereus and his sister (16:15).*

9. List the persons sending greetings to Rome who are with Paul at the time of writing. (16:21-23)

> *1. Timothy (16:21); 2. Lucius (16:21); 3. Jason (16:21); 4. Sosipater (16:21); 5. Tertius (16:22); 6. Gaius (16:23); 7. Erastus (16:23); 8. Quartus (16:23).*

10. Estimate the proportion of women to men among the church leaders Paul mentions in 16:1-23.

> *Ten out of thirty-seven (about 27 percent) of the church leaders are women: Phoebe, Priscilla, Mary, Junia, Tryphena, Tryphosa, Persis, Rufus's mother, Julia, and Nereus's sister.*

DIMENSION TWO:
WHAT DOES THE BIBLE MEAN?

The reason we are studying the material in Romans 14–16 in our third lesson is to complete the picture of the situation in Rome. Our effort to overcome theological abstraction in dealing with Romans means that a vivid picture of the situation in Rome must be kept in mind. The information concerning this situation is at the end of the letter, which requires a somewhat backward procedure for studying Romans.

The material in 14:1–15:13 is the culmination of the theological and ethical argument in Romans. These sections provide ethical guidelines for living in righteousness, thus developing the major theme of Romans 1:16-17. In these final chapters, we find evidence to identify who the weak and the strong were in Rome and also discover the direction of Paul's argument in response to their controversy. In 14:13-23, Paul develops guidelines for mutual upbuilding in the house churches. Righteousness is defined in these verses as the mutual acceptance and growth that unites rather than destroys the church.

In 15:1-6, Paul describes Christ as the model for the interaction between the groups in the church. In particular, edifying the "weak" is stressed in these verses, possibly because they are in a vulnerable position because the strong are in the majority.

Finally, Paul brings to a conclusion his formal argument in Romans (15:7-13). He begins with a summary in verse 7 of the tolerant argument concerning the weak and the strong; then Paul gives a series of Scripture quotations that bear on the question of the motivation and the horizon of the world mission. The emphasis on the Gentiles in this section was observed by the group members as they answered Question 5 in Dimension One indicating the scope of Paul's argument in Romans in providing a rationale for world mission and unification. The promise given to Abraham, that in him all the nations would be blessed, is here brought to its fitting conclusion.

The Weak and the Strong

Traditional Bible commentaries present one of three views identifying the weak and the strong in these verses. The material I have written provides a fourth alternative, so clarifying the other options may help.

The traditional and most widely stated view is that the weak are the Jewish Christians, and the strong are Gentile Christians. Some details in the argument fit this view quite well. Some of the actions characteristic of the weak would be typical of Jewish Christians who remained true to the Torah.

Actions Characteristic of the "Weak"

14:2—"eats only vegetables"

14:5—"considers one day more sacred than another"

14:6—"regards one day as special"

14:14—believes something may be "unclean in itself"

14:21—refrains from "meat" and "wine"

In addition, Paul's strong identification of himself with the Gentile Christians in Romans 15:1 as well as in 14:14 would serve to confirm this traditional view. I can see some difficult barriers to holding this view, however.

First and foremost, we have no convincing evidence that conservative Jewish Christians were vegetarians, that they refrained from meat and wine. There is some evidence of fringe groups who tended toward asceticism, and it is understandable at certain times that Jewish groups in the

Gentile world who did not have access to kosher butcher shops might temporarily refrain from meat. But that they would do so even on the great Jewish festival of the Passover is unthinkable. That they would refrain from wine at such a time is also difficult to believe.

This traditional view also labors under the burden that some of the Jewish Christians mentioned in Romans 16 had worked closely with Paul and in all probability shared his theology, which was closer to the strong than to the weak. Priscilla and Aquila can be mentioned here. It is likely also that a number of the persons that we identified in Question 6 in Dimension One as closely related to Paul in his previous mission would have stood in this theological tradition as well and thought of themselves as strong.

An elaborate refinement of this traditional view is found in a book by Paul S. Minear, *The Obedience of Faith: The Purposes of Paul in the Epistle to the Romans* (SCM Press, 1971). Minear infers five groups from the evidence in Romans 14:1–16:27:

1. *"The 'weak in faith' who condemned the 'strong in faith'"* are viewed as consisting largely of converted Jews and a few Gentiles who had accepted the law when they became Christians.

2. *"The 'strong in faith' who scorned and despised the 'weak in faith'"* were uncircumcised Gentiles or Jews who relished the liberty that they had in Christ. They felt free from religious taboos because of their powerful experiences of conversion, and they despised persons who did not feel free to join in their celebration.

3. *"The doubters"* are viewed by Minear as persons coming from groups 1 and 2 who were unsure of their position and tended to waver between the extremes. Minear finds a reference to them in 14:23.

4. *"The 'weak in faith' who did not condemn 'the strong'"* are identified with those in the congregation who accepted Paul's argument and remained true to their Jewish-Christian convictions.

5. *"The 'strong in faith' who did not despise the 'weak'"* are identified as Paul's disciples who come primarily from the Gentile Christian background, though some Jews were included. These last two groups accepted Paul's argument and were tolerant toward other people.

The difficulty of this analysis is that it is poorly coordinated with the evidence concerning the five house churches in Rome that is found in Romans 16. In fact, as far as evidence of group life is concerned, only groups 1 and 2 are actually evident in Romans. Groups 4 and 5 are purely hypothetical because Minear simply assumes that some people among the so-called "weak" and "strong" accepted Paul's argument. Group 3 is not a proper group at all, since it consists of persons from other groups who are doubting their convictions. As a consequence, no other scholars have accepted Minear's elaborate proposal.

The third approach to the Roman house church situation is to assume that no clear identification is possible because of the peculiar quality of Paul's argument. Scholars who view Romans as a doctrinal treatise and stress the generality and general application of the argument sometimes tend in this direction. One scholar who takes this point of view, for example, argues that Paul is intentionally vague and self-contradictory in the details that he gives concerning the weak in Romans 14. This scholar says that Paul's purpose is to make an argument so general that it will fit a wide range of church situations. This presupposes that Romans is not really directed to a specific church situation but is a more general epistle aimed at providing guidance for a wide range of churches in the ancient as well as in the modern world.

The difficulty with this approach is that peculiar circumstances in the Roman house churches after the edict of Claudius are not taken into account. The evidence from Romans 14:1–15:7 that Gentile Christians are now in charge and that Jewish Christians are having a difficult time finding a place would fit the circumstances of a return after the time of exile was over. Nor does this approach take any account of Romans 16. Most scholars who follow this approach believe that Romans 16, in fact, was not directed to Rome at all but was a note sent to some other churches or to another church in particular, Ephesus. We will discuss later, briefly, the problem of the authenticity of Romans 16.

The viewpoint presented in this lesson is worked out in detail in my book *Christian Tolerance: Paul's Message to the Modern Church* (Westminster Press, 1982). I suggest that Paul defines the weak and strong in consciously broad categories, thus encompassing a range of congregational options within the extremes.

> The catchwords "weak" and "strong" that Paul employs . . . are highly misleading in their modern connotation, implying that the distinction had to do with weakness or strength of convictions and will power. Actually, as the research on this issue has made plain, the terms had probably been imposed by the "strong" who identified their superiority in terms of spiritual courage to defy traditional scruples. Rather than supposing that the "strong" comprised a single group, we may appropriately think of this term as roughly equivalent with "liberal" in the modern political sense, depicting a fairly wide range of ideological, racial, and temperamental differences. Similarly the "weak" should be thought of as roughly equivalent with "conservative," consisting of various groups of Jewish and Gentile Christians favoring a scrupulous attitude toward the Jewish law and certain liturgical and ascetic practices (pages 29-30).

I link this identification of the weak and the strong with the circumstances of the two years prior to Paul's writing the letter in which the Jewish Christians were allowed to return and conflicts over leadership developed between liberals and conservatives, old and new Christians, charismatics and traditionalists. I argue that "the controversies undoubtedly crossed racial lines because there were Jewish Christians who inclined toward the Pauline view of freedom from the law and others who were loyal to the more conservative pattern of Peter and the Jerusalem mother church." The Gentile side probably included some of a conservative stripe, likely associated with the two house churches within the Roman bureaucracies, those belonging to Aristobulus (16:10) and to Narcissus (16:11). I feel the Letter to the Romans must be placed within this tangled situation.

Romans 14:1-4. Romans 14:1 indicates that the strong who are in the majority position have accepted the weak only on the premise that they could successfully convince them to change their minds. The "disputable matters" are defined in subsequent verses as relating to food laws, the cultic calendar, and theology. In 14:3 the distinctive strategy to enforce conformity used by both sides is described. Apparently, the strong, or the liberals, are "treat[ing] with contempt" those who are not able to join them at their level of freedom. The weak, or conservatives, are "judg[ing]" those who do not live up to their high moral standards, and this judgment is the cause of quarreling. The likelihood that these are the distinctive strategies to enforce conformity being used in Rome is strengthened by the fact that Paul restates his case with slightly different language in 14:10. In 14:1, *quarreling* is used in a more inclusive sense to describe the behavior of both sides.

The question "Who are you to judge someone else's servant?" (verse 4) clearly alludes to the behavior of both the conservatives and the liberals. Both are acting toward their competitors as if they were the lord of the other. The "master" in verse 4 is clearly God.

Romans 14:5-6. In 14:5, Paul refers to "consider[ing] one day more sacred than another," which is a reference to feast days, fast days, and the Sabbath. The conservatives spoke of a day being more sacred than another in that they saw the day as designated by God for a specific kind of activity. The persons who consider "every day alike" are obviously the liberals who have abandoned the cultic calendar of Judaism as well as, perhaps, the special feast days of the Greco-Roman world. In verses 5-6, Paul subtly equalizes the claims of both the conservatives and the liberals. The argument is that as long as each side acts in response to the Lord, their behavior must be supported and applauded by the others.

Romans 14:15-16. In these verses Paul deals with liberals causing conservatives to violate their standards by acting in ways that they really feel are inappropriate. In verse 16, Paul deals with the discrediting of freedom when it is used to cause the downfall of others. That which is "good" for the liberal is the freedom that she or he has in Christ.

Romans 14:22-23. The literal translation of verse 22 is as follows:

Keep the faith that you have in accordance with yourself in the presence of God.
Blessed is the one who does not judge himself by what he approved.

This verse is addressed primarily to those who are in danger of abandoning their convictions. Belief is defined here as an internal standard that each person must follow. Shakespeare stated the essential theme of this verse in the words, "To thine own self be true." Paul does not issue a command for privacy but rather for integrity. In this sense, 14:23 should be understood to mean that any act that does not proceed from your own belief violates your integrity and therefore is a sin. This standard needs to be followed by both liberals and conservatives in Rome.

Romans 15:1. I would render 15:1 differently from the NIV:

We the powerful are obligated to bear the weaknesses of the powerless and not to please ourselves.

The NIV refers to "the failings of the weak." This phrase seems to imply that the conservatives have an ethical flaw or a lack of will power. I believe that a proper translation suggests that those who are liberal should bear with those who are conservative. On the basis of Paul's previous argument, he would not wish to place either side in a negative light.

Romans 15:5-13. In 15:5-6 and 15:13, Paul draws together his argument with powerful benedictions, expressing his desires for the congregation and the burden of his previous argument. The first benediction summarizes mainly the material from Romans 14:1–15:4. The second draws together the argument of the entire letter. The hope that is lifted up here is for the unification of the world through the gospel. The centrality of the Gentile mission for the entire Letter of Romans is magnificently caught by the series of scriptural quotations (15:9-12) that lead up to the final benediction.

Romans 16:3-16. Phoebe's activities require the support of the leaders of the Roman house churches, which is why Paul moves immediately from recommending her (16:1-2) to greeting all the church leaders in Rome. The work that your group has done answering Questions 6, 7, and 8 in Dimension One brings forth the material necessary for this discussion. Paul greets fifteen persons with whom he has worked earlier, only a few of whom appear to be actually attached to house churches. Since Paul knows them intimately, he probably can expect their cooperation in the Spanish mission. Some of these people are Christians of long standing. Andronicus and Junia are Jewish Christians who, according to 16:7, became leaders prior to Paul's conversion. So they had been Christians at least since AD 34. Their reputation and activities go back more than twenty years in the rapidly developing early church.

The thirteen leaders whose names Paul knows by hearsay are also needed to provide support for the Spanish mission. The resources of each of the five house churches would be required to make this mission successful. The Roman administrators in the houses of Aristobulus and Narcissus involved in the imperial correspondence would be equally adept at Latin and at Greek. This would place them in an excellent position to provide translation resources and to make recommendations for traveling companions who would be able to understand what was happening in Spain. The other three house churches mentioned would be just as significant a resource for the Spanish mission, but Paul would need the advice and counsel of these two churches in particular.

Paul has no difficulty in working with Phoebe, who, given the class structure of the Greco-Roman world, would clearly have been perceived as the senior partner in any collaborative mission with a person of Paul's social standing. The fact that ten of the thirty-seven persons that Paul greets in 16:1-23 are women indicates the openness to resources from females that marked the first generation of the Christian mission.

Romans 16:17-27. The textual history of Romans 16 is quite tangled and probably should not be raised unless someone asks about it. Here are the essential details in case the question is raised. The major problem is that the Greek manuscripts we have of Romans place the final benediction of 16:25-27 at a number of locations. Some of the other benedictions and greetings are also located at different spots, which has led text critics to the conclusion that at least three forms of Romans circulated in the ancient world:

1. A fourteen-chapter letter that ended with the benediction of 16:25-27 placed at the end of Chapter 14;

2. A fifteen-chapter letter with the benediction of 15:33 concluding the letter; and

3. A sixteen-chapter letter with the benediction in its current location.

Given the fact that one of our manuscripts deletes the word *Rome* from the opening chapter of the letter, it seems clear that some versions of this letter circulated as general epistles. Many scholars have inferred from this that Romans was written by Paul in at least two forms, a fifteen-chapter letter addressed to Rome and a sixteen-chapter letter with a final note and greetings directed to Ephesus where many of the people mentioned here were known to have resided. Research has made this theory less likely, however; and one problem in supporting this last theory is how Paul could have mentioned so many names without personal greetings if this were sent to an area where Paul had worked as long as he had in Ephesus. So current scholarly opinion tends to conclude that Paul sent Romans as a sixteen-chapter letter to Rome.

The material in 16:17-20 is highly controversial and disputed. In the event that members of your group have an interest in this material, here are some of the pros and cons. The suggestion that these verses were inserted by the early church that edited the Pauline letters rests on several observations. These verses break the flow of the argument and are completely out of the mood of the friendly greetings surrounding them. Romans 16:16 and 16:21 would be smoothly connected if these verses were eliminated. The mood of mutual cooperation and tolerance that this chapter conveys, particularly when one considers that Paul is treating as equals the members of all five house churches, is seriously disrupted by this warning against heretics.

The language inside these verses is also quite different from that used elsewhere in Romans and in the other authentic Pauline letters. The recommendation that persons "who cause divisions and put obstacles in your way that are contrary to the teaching you have learned" should be avoided flatly contradicts the argument of 14:1–15:13. Nowhere else in the Pauline letters does Paul make doctrinal conformity the crucial indication of legitimacy as in these verses. The vicious personal attack of 16:18 is also unparalleled in the authentic Pauline letters. This verse is reminiscent, however, of the way the Pastoral Epistles deal with their opponents. Verse 19 is also unusual for Paul in that obedience is used here without reference to the term *faith*, with which it is connected at every other point in Romans. Here pure obedience to whatever Paul says is defined as the line dividing good from evil. This view is vastly different from the one in Romans 12:1-3.

Finally, the hope expressed in verse 20 that God will crush heretics in the form of Satan "under your feet" is far from the spirit of the cooperative letter that Paul has written. This wording encourages Christians to believe that their opponents are satanic and ought to be destroyed. These words, of course, were enacted with great effectiveness during the time of the Inquisition.

Many commentators, however, believe that these words are an authentic part of Paul's letter, establishing the limits beyond which tolerance should not go. Whatever position you or the members of your group come to, it is important to keep in mind that 16:17-20 is part of the canonical letter. There have been times in the Christian tradition when the application of these verses has become necessary. The key question that needs to be discussed, therefore, is which side of Paul's argument in Romans is more appropriate for the local church and the circumstances that you are facing. Is it the open-minded cooperation and the tolerance of diverse viewpoints in Romans 1–15 and the friendly greeting of the rest of Romans 16? Or is it, because of peculiar circumstances, the hard line of Romans 16:17-20? What is appropriate for the Christian ethic has to do with circumstances and the moment. One cannot decide which approach ought to be used in every situation.

DIMENSION THREE: WHAT DOES THE BIBLE MEAN TO ME?

Conservatives and Liberals

We are struck by the parallels between the ancient situation in Rome and that of modern congregations. The tensions between rich and poor churches is not only an embarrassment to the church but also in all probability a hindrance to its mission as well. The Letter to the Romans encourages us to think of the task of cooperation as an essential ingredient to mission. In Paul's circumstances, mounting the mission to Spain was not possible without the resources of all the house churches. There may well be circumstances in the modern world and certainly in local congregations where something similar could be said.

Making a Conscious Effort to Accept

Paul is seeking to enlist all the potential leaders in one cooperative effort. The tensions between those leaders, which we can only partially reconstruct, sound very much like the tensions between leaders in modern churches as well.

Pluralism

The pluralism manifest in the five house churches in Rome has many modern parallels. The church does not always require the same structure and leadership pattern, if the model of Romans is to be trusted. These relatively small house churches, perhaps comparable to church school classes or prayer cells in modern churches, became the vital centers of growth and spiritual development. The Letter to the Romans has a promise and hope that such can become the case today as well.

These three issues are intertwined. Our theological (and political) stances can easily put us at odds with those whose stances are different. Our cultural viewpoints can make us quarrel with or be resistant to others who come from other cultures. How can persons of faith maintain personal religious integrity and still live in harmony within a divided and pluralistic church and society?

I am not ashamed of the gospel, because it is the power of God that brings salvation to everyone who believes (1:16).

4

RIGHTEOUSNESS AND WRATH

Romans 1:16–2:16

DIMENSION ONE: WHAT DOES THE BIBLE SAY?

Answer these questions by reading Romans 1:16–2:16

1. In the thesis statement of 1:16-17, what does Paul identify as the "power of God," and where is the "righteousness of God" revealed?

    Both the "power of God" and the "righteousness of God" are linked to the gospel.

2. Where have God's invisible attributes been seen? (1:20)

    They are seen in "what has been made."

3. What are the consequences of refusing to acknowledge and glorify God? (1:21-22)

    Those who refuse to honor God become futile in their thinking, and "their foolish hearts [are] darkened."

4. How many times does Paul repeat that God "gave over" the wicked to the consequences of their deeds? (1:24-28)

    Paul says three times that God "gave them over" to the consequences of their sin, in 1:24, 26, and 28.

5. Does Paul describe "shameful lusts" as the cause or the consequence of divine wrath? (1:26-27)

    The phrase "God gave them over to . . ." indicates that shameful lusts are the consequence of divine wrath, not its cause.

6. How many forms of evil does Paul list? (1:29-31)

> *Paul lists twenty-one forms of evil, starting with "wickedness" in verse 29 and ending with having "no mercy" in verse 31.*

7. On the basis of the wording of 2:5-10, is *wrath* in this section a present experience or a future expectation?

> *The idea of "storing up wrath" in verse 5 implies a future "day of God's wrath." The future tense of the verbs "will repay" (2:6), "will give" (2:7), and "there will be" (2:8, 9) indicates that it is the future wrath that Paul has in mind here.*

8. How many times is the expression "first for the Jew, then for the Gentile" repeated in 1:16–2:11?

> *Paul repeats this phrase three times, in 1:16; 2:9, 10.*

9. Who is "righteous in God's sight"? (2:13)

> *"Those who obey the law" are righteous before God.*

10. What does Paul say about the Gentiles who do not have the law? (2:14-15)

> *The Gentiles who do not have the law yet follow it do so by listening to their conscience and thoughts.*

DIMENSION TWO:
WHAT DOES THE BIBLE MEAN?

Romans 1:16–2:16 begins the abstract, formal argument of the letter. Teaching this material presents a series of challenges. It is quite important that you devise a plan for your discussion of this material that avoids getting bogged down in tiny details but that nevertheless remains true enough to the flow of the argument that Paul's point is understood.

Keeping in mind that Paul is making a case throughout this letter for the unification of Jews and Gentiles, for the mission of the gospel, and for its world-transforming power may help you in dealing with this highly abstract argument.

Romans 1:17. English provides two different words for what in the original text of Romans was a single family of terms. We speak of *righteousness* and *justification*, both of which have different forms and rather different connotations in English. The difficulty is particularly seen in 1:17. For instance, the King James Version translates this verse, "For therein is the righteousness of God revealed from faith to faith. . . . The just shall live by faith." The problem is that the word *just* comes from exactly the same stem as the term *righteousness*.

When this translation problem is not understood, as is often the case, "justification by faith alone" gets entirely separated from the "righteousness of God." That is, God's activity in transforming humans is understood basically as the gift of forgiveness that allows us to be "justified" even though we have violated the law. But being justified is different from being righteous. In fact, Paul wishes to speak of humans in this entire letter as being *rightwised*, that is, "to make right, to set one right, and to achieve a transformation in which humans come to reflect the righteousness of God."

Group members may have difficulty defining *righteousness* and connecting it with their previous understanding of *justification*. A simple set of alternatives can be suggested here. An old-fashioned view is that *righteousness* is the standard for what is right for God as well as for humans. When this interpretation of righteousness becomes central, it leads to a moralistic understanding of what human salvation means. It can end up in a new form of the law, a major problem for Romans. That is, people can be led to think that if they simply conform to the high standards of the Christian faith, they are justified.

Another approach was shaped, in particular, by Martin Luther. In this tradition, *justification* or *rightwising* is understood to be the gift of freedom from condemnation. The difficulty with this interpretation, whether in its moralistic or abstract theological form, is that the parallel Paul wishes to create in Romans 1:17 between the righteousness of God and the "rightwising" of humans is lost sight of.

The viewpoint I am following in this course is that the "righteousness of God" in Romans refers to God's capacity to impose righteousness on the world. God has a claim on the creation that it reflect divine righteousness. Thus when Paul speaks of the "righteousness of God" as being "revealed," he is operating out of the Jewish tradition of God standing triumphant at the end of history, having vanquished or transformed all foes. This view lets us see the close parallel between the righteousness of God and the righteousness given to humans. When humans are caught up in the divine plan and made to conform to the divine will, they enter into a relationship with God that has righteousness as its major component. They achieve the goal for which they were created.

When communities are caught up in the righteousness from God, they become agents of the divine will over the whole created order. Thus the biblical idea that the fall of humankind led to the fall of the creation, to the distortion of ecology, to the destruction of the planet itself, is all caught up in Paul's notion in Romans. Paul hopes to offer a concept of the gospel that trusts the will of God to regain control over the whole world. In this way a basis is provided for a world mission that not only transforms persons but also ultimately transforms the principalities and powers and regains and restores the lost world itself. So, when Paul refers to "the righteousness of God," he is close to the Old Testament idea that the "glory of God" is manifest when God wins a victory over enemies.

One of the difficult issues in 1:19-32 is that of "natural revelation." The argument in these verses is that all humans have the capacity to recognize God by seeing what God has created. Many commentaries that were shaped by the neoorthodox tradition of the 1920s through 1950s were highly sensitive on the issue of natural revelation. Some of these commentators tried to downplay Paul's argument at this point.

Current scholars see that Paul in fact makes use of a widespread tradition of natural revelation that was typical of the Greco-Roman world as a whole and also of some Jewish theologians. Paul's argument in these verses reminds me of an idea that was widely shared in Greco-Roman culture, namely that an original stage of human existence and history allowed humans to see God's nature clearly and visibly. The second stage, the fall of the human race, came with the deterioration of humans and the rise of corrupt priests at temples that confused the divine image with nature itself.

The whole question of how God is visible in nature is a vital one for the Greco-Roman world and for Paul. A widespread assumption among serious religious thinkers in a place like Rome was that true worship should be a matter of contemplating the heavens and the earth and therefore cultivating a knowledge of what God was like. These ideas were picked up by the late Jewish thinkers so that quite likely Paul operated out of a double tradition as he wrote these words. For example, in the Apocrypha (NRSV), the Wisdom of Solomon 13:5 suggests that "from the greatness and beauty of created things / comes a corresponding perception of their Creator." The idea here is precisely that which Paul argues, namely that God's attributes are visible in the created things.

Nowhere else in the Greco-Roman world or in Judaism do we have so strong an emphasis as here on the conscious repudiation of the knowledge of God on the part of humans. Paul's emphasis on suppressing the truth about God as the essence of sin and his contention that humans tend to confuse themselves with the divine sets off Paul from his contemporaries. The radical side of his idea of natural revelation that is consciously perverted by humans can best be explained on the basis of Paul's theology of the cross.

Paul discovered in the Christ event the depth of human perversion and twistedness, the tendency of humans to reject the truth and to deny its validity for their lives, even to the point of killing the Christ when they had him in their grasp.

Romans 1:29-32. As the participant book makes plain, the problem of the human race, according to 1:19-32, is far more than a matter of breaking the law. It is more serious than breaking religious principles. It is instead the tendency to rebel and to repress the truth about the distinction between creatures and their Creator. Therefore, when you teach this material, be on the alert to avoid drifting into petty moralism. The moral features that Paul discusses in this passage are the consequences and results of basic human sin rather than its form. In fact, most of what is preached against as sin in Christian tradition, material such as Romans 1:26-31, is the result of something much more basic.

When we understand Paul's argument that humans have the knowledge of God but refuse to allow God to be God, falling into twistedness and darkness of mind, the parallel in the Hebrew Scriptures becomes particularly plain. The participant book refers to the garden of Eden story, which is highly relevant for this passage.

In addition, you may wish to throw light on 1:23 by referring to the golden calf episode in Exodus 32. In that story humans felt uncomfortable with the absent and invisible God and set about to create an image that would provide them the fertility and prosperity they hoped to gain. Exodus 32 shows that idolatry, the making of "images made to look like a mortal human being and birds and animals and reptiles" (Romans 1:23), is rooted in the human yearning to achieve goals by manipulating God. Therefore I find it significant that Paul follows the logic of Exodus 32 in Romans.

After the Hebrews had created the golden calf, they danced about it and fell into a sexual orgy that was so destructive and noisy that it brought Moses back from the distant mountain. Similarly, in the argument here in Romans, sexual perversion, the free expression of the human will to dominate and to destroy, is the consequence of creating finite images for God and making God into nothing more than a projection of human desires.

The issue of twistedness, particularly the distortion of human sexual relations that one sees in 1:24-27, is likely to be of particular interest to some members of your group because of debates over the issue of homosexuality. One fundamental observation is needed to keep this kind of discussion in context. Paul is describing what he perceives as the consequence of human confusion between the divine and the finite. And he is operating out of a widespread tradition in his own Hebrew culture that sexual perversions are fundamentally a violation of the will of the Creator.

Given the divisiveness over the issue of homosexuality and the heated feelings that it can evoke in the church today, you would do well to steer away from this topic unless well-informed resources are at hand to help throw light on it. It is certainly not crucial for an understanding of Paul's argument to come to an agreement on what the current status of homosexuality ought to be in the church. No matter what decision is made on that, it seems to me that Paul's basic argument still remains true, namely that when humans confuse themselves with God and try to suppress the truth about themselves, they fall into various forms of twistedness.

Romans 2:6-7, 13-16. One of the most difficult puzzles about Romans 2:6-7 is that it appears to contradict the basic teaching of Romans, namely that humans are "rightwised" by faith alone. Particularly when one takes the thesis of Romans into account (1:16-17), the statement that God will "repay each person according to what they have done" (2:6) is quite puzzling. This puzzle is deepened with 2:13, which states that "it is those who obey the law who will be declared righteous" (will be "rightwised").

Many commentaries on Romans deal with these seeming contradictions by evading the clear force of what Paul says. One approach is to suggest that these verses deal merely with a theoretical possibility. If it is true that all persons sin, then we cannot say that we will be justified according to our works. These commentaries say that Paul, for the sake of a theoretical argument, develops here a purely theoretical option. This argument is hard to sustain in light of the direct references to the Roman audience in 2:5, 7-8. We do not get the impression from these lines that Paul is dealing with something that was not present in Rome.

A second evasive approach is to suggest that Paul is dealing only with Christian believers in this passage. In this way Paul can be seen as condemning non-Christians but suggesting that those who really have been transformed by the gospel have been rendered capable of producing works and therefore achieving salvation. But that Paul is dealing strictly with a Christian audience in these verses is flatly contradicted by 2:9-10, in which the phrase "first for the Jew, then for the Gentile" is repeated.

Perhaps Paul meant to leave open some loopholes in his earlier argument. And perhaps the statement about the righteous Gentile in Romans 2 makes it possible for Christians to recognize persons outside the Christian faith and even outside the Judeo-Christian tradition whose lives nevertheless have a degree of authenticity and goodness that seems difficult to dispute.

Romans 2:11. Studies in Romans have made us more aware of the crucial significance of Paul's argument that God shows no favoritism (2:11). This element is essential in the issue we have just discussed, namely whether God will accept those who have never heard the Christian gospel or the Jewish faith, those who have never heard or perceived the Jewish law but nevertheless perform it (2:13-16). An investigation by Professor Jouette M. Bassler of Georgetown University (*Divine Impartiality: Paul and a Theological Axiom*; Scholars' Press, 1982) shows the unusual way in which Paul has developed this traditional Jewish concept.

Of particular interest in Professor Bassler's study is the realization that the social consequence of God's impartial treatment of Jews and Gentiles is "that no distinction is to be made within the community itself." She also writes that God's impartial acceptance of the two groups expands to include mutual acceptance between the two groups. At this point her study is closely linked to the approach I take in this course on Romans. My aim is to show that at crucial points in Paul's argument, even points that sound abstract to the modern reader, Paul is addressing tensions within the Roman house churches. Paul's argument about the impartiality of God stands as a hedge against the competitive spirit among those house churches who believed that each had the total truth and that the other side was wrong.

God is not the possession of the weak or of the strong. We could also say that God is not the possession of the United Methodists or the Southern Baptists or the Roman Catholics or the Greek Orthodox. God is absolutely impartial. God treats persons of all races and nations and religions with a fair standard of performance. Until the Roman house churches understood this, they would not be able to overcome their tensions and cooperate in a mission to the world. And any gospel they would have for the world would be fatally flawed if it rested on the premise, often followed in the mission thrust of later Christianity, that one group has a corner on the truth and is therefore superior to others.

That kind of mission is nothing more than a vicious form of imperialism. And any such imperialism was bound to be rejected by the Spaniards who had already suffered so much from Roman imperialism that they would be unlikely to adopt another form.

DIMENSION THREE:
WHAT DOES THE BIBLE MEAN TO ME?

The Gospel and the Power of God

Note Paul's emphases mentioned in the second paragraph of Dimension Two: the unification of Jews and Gentiles in the house churches, the mission of the gospel (specifically to Spain), and the world-transforming power of God. We might think about God's power in terms of its personal nature (unification), its practical nature (mission to Spain), and its universal nature (transforming the world). Another way to frame this, using Paul's example in Romans, might be to think of the ultimate intention of God (transformation), the intentional plan in bringing about transformation (mission to Spain), and the immediate or initial steps to work the plan (unification).

Think about God's transforming power, revealed in the gospel, in terms of a local issue, situation, or crisis. In that situation, how might (or could) you see God's intention or practical application of the gospel message? What personal and/or initial steps must be addressed? What might be the possible consequences if God's power is seen and acted upon as God reveals it?

Justification and Righteousness

Help the group sort out the language and theological issues presented here by *justification* and *righteousness* and the added terms *rightwised* and *just*. Identify in those terms what is the activity of God, what is the activity of humankind, and how they interconnect.

Conflict and Impartiality

Paul gets to the heart of the quarreling among congregations immediately after greeting them. Read through Romans 2. Identify and list all the specific issues that Paul elevates as evidence of this quarreling. Some are specific (as in his mention of the law) and others are general (as in passing judgment). Take as impartial a look as you can at the current religious landscape in the United States, both between Christian churches and their theological spectrum and between Christian and non-Christian religions. (This is a huge range for consideration, so you might take it in at least two segments.) What examples do you see as evidence of "quarreling" or passing judgment? Does this (or how does this) come under God's judgment? In what ways do we show or claim favoritism in a way that God may find wanting? What does or could happen when we suspend our judgment or cease claiming and showing favoritism?

You, then, who teach others, do you not teach yourself? You who preach against stealing, do you steal? (2:21).

RELIGION PERVERTED
Romans 2:17–3:20

DIMENSION ONE:
WHAT DOES THE BIBLE SAY?

Answer these questions by reading Romans 2:17–3:20

1. How many claims of religious superiority does Paul list, and what are they? (2:17-20)

    Paul makes ten claims in these verses: (1) relying on the law (2:17); (2) bragging on one's relationship to God (2:17); (3) knowing the will of God (2:18); (4) approving what is superior (2:18); (5) being instructed in the law (2:18); (6) acting as a guide for the blind (2:19); (7) being a light for those in darkness (2:19); (8) instructing the foolish (2:20); (9) teaching little children (2:20); and (10) having the embodiment of knowledge and truth in the law (2:20).

2. How many rhetorical questions does Paul ask in 2:21-23?

    Paul asks five questions—two in verse 21, two in verse 22, and one in verse 23.

3. How is Paul's quotation of Isaiah 52:5 different from the original? (2:24; Isaiah 52:5)

    That God's name is blasphemed in Isaiah 52:5 is due to the Exile, in which "my people have been taken away for nothing." In Romans 2:24, Paul says God's name is blasphemed because Israel sins.

4. What does Paul argue about the value of circumcision? (2:25-26)

    Paul claims circumcision has value only if one actually observes the law. Otherwise, the circumcised Jews are no better than uncircumcised Gentiles.

5. How does Paul define the "real Jew"? (2:28-29)

    The "real Jew" has the "inward" circumcision of the heart, "by the Spirit, not by the written code."

6. How many rhetorical questions does Paul ask in 3:1-9?

The New International Version has ten rhetorical questions asked by Paul.

7. What word that is not in Psalms 14:1-3 and 53:1-3 does Paul use in quoting these psalms? (3:10-12)

Paul uses the word righteous *in quoting these psalms.*

8. Who does Paul say will be held accountable to God? (3:19)

Paul writes that "the whole world [will be] held accountable to God."

DIMENSION TWO: WHAT DOES THE BIBLE MEAN?

The material in this lesson is full of dangers as well as of promise. In a culture with a record of some anti-Semitism, it is particularly dangerous to discuss Paul's effort to show that Jews as well as Gentiles are involved in sin. Paul's conversation partners here included Jewish Christians in Rome rather than Jews who have never received the gospel. We therefore need to assume that this argument is within the Christian community, not between Christians and unconverted Jews.

Paul hoped to lead the house churches in Rome to a more realistic assessment of their situation. If you are convinced that you have earned grace, that you are in a superior position, you will never be able to understand the pure gift of grace. Only those who are empty can be filled. Only those who acknowledge their need can be helped. Therefore this material has a tremendous relevance for the Christian faith. But its dangers when used in preaching against other religions must constantly be kept in mind.

This lesson begins in the middle of the section of Paul's argument that deals with impartial judgment according to deeds. That section runs from Romans 2:1 to 2:29. Our lesson begins with the second half, beginning with verse 17, the material that deals specifically with the claims of the religious elite. Paul concentrates in these verses on the "Jews," by which he has in mind primarily the Jewish Christians who are struggling against Gentile Christians in Rome. Paul's contention throughout this entire section is that all persons, Jews as well as Gentiles, are involved in sin and that all persons, whether Jews or Gentiles, will be treated impartially and fairly by God. There are no exemptions. The severity of the argument here is designed to uncover the worst perversion of all, the perversion of religion into a system of superiority.

Romans 2:17-23. One of the remarkable features of 2:17-20 is that Paul does not finish the sentence. This incomplete sentence is somewhat disguised in the NIV and other modern translations where a dash appears at the end of verse 20. The impression is given that the sentence continues in verse 21. In fact, verse 21 in the Greek begins a new sentence; and modern scholars believe that Paul left the long sentence of verses 17-20 unfinished on purpose. One of the studies on this problem suggests that Paul wishes to express here what is too horrible to express completely, namely the fullness of human arrogance and the final perversion of the great religious heritage of the Hebrew Scriptures. He leaves the sentence incomplete because it is impossible to complete. When a great religious heritage is perverted into a system of superiority claims, the heritage becomes its unspeakable opposite.

In Paul's effort to show a scandalous excess of religious pride, he does not wish to subvert the proper use of that same religion. He forms his argument with some rather elaborate plays on the sacred numbers of Judaism. As we see from answering Question 1 in Dimension One, Paul lists ten claims in the incomplete sentence. This matches the Ten Commandments. In the next section, 2:21-23, Paul asks five questions, matching the five books of Moses.

Romans 2:25-29. Circumcision had been under dispute within Christian groups in the seven or eight years before Paul wrote Romans. The opening phase of this dispute is reflected in Acts 15:1 when Luke reports that "certain people came down from Judea to Antioch and were teaching the believers: 'Unless you are circumcised, according to the custom taught by Moses, you cannot be saved.'"

Paul had struggled over this issue in the Apostolic Conference (Galatians 2:1-10), and it may have been an issue also to some degree among the churches in Rome. Circumcision as the sign of the covenant and as the proof of one's membership in the "seed of Abraham" was one of the most important features in the claim of moral and religious superiority on the part of Jewish Christians. That circumcision was seen as necessary for salvation is clear in Acts 15:1. We have no indications from the Jewish community that they saw circumcision as necessary for salvation. As far as Jews were concerned, circumcision was simply a sign of membership in the community of the law. Faithfulness to this law insured that the person would continue in the realm of salvation as far as Jewish theology was concerned. But in the Christian community circumcision was being used as a sign of superiority of one group over the other. This misuse is what Paul counters in these verses.

Paul says that obedience to the law is what makes circumcision significant. The "true Jew" in this sense is the one who has accepted the law of God and obeys it from the heart. The effect of this argument is to make circumcision subordinate to the larger purposes of the law of God. The heart of the argument is that the "true Jews" are the just persons of every race. Whoever does the will of God from the heart is a proper Jew. Thus the claims of being superior that groups in Rome are holding over one another are defused.

Finally, in 3:1-9, Paul lists ten rhetorical questions. This structuring of the argument in groups of fives and tens indicates the degree to which he wishes to appeal to those who are loyal to the Hebrew tradition. He bases his case on the same Scripture, the same tradition, that is being perverted by religious pride in Rome. The Scripture is not at fault; human sin is.

The Citation of Scripture

Consistent with his effort to rest his case on the Scripture and tradition that have been perverted in Rome, Paul cites a number of scriptural passages in the section we are studying this week. A word of warning might be stated here. Finding the exact equivalent of the translation of Paul's citations in our translation of the Old Testament is difficult. Paul's citations come from the Greek translation of the Hebrew that had slight variations from the Hebrew. In some instances it now appears to textual critics that the Greek tradition of the Septuagint (Greek translation of the Old Testament) Paul was citing may well have been in existence in Hebrew at the time Paul wrote. Some of the Hebrew Old Testament evolved after the time of Paul's writing, and in several instances we can find examples of the rabbis altering the Hebrew text in a direction away from that which was being favored by Christian use.

At any event, it is important to see that Paul has the free attitude toward the Hebrew Scriptures that was characteristic of the other scholars of his time. Sometimes he quotes exactly from the Septuagint. At other times he changes the Scriptures, sometimes quite drastically, in order to fit his current circumstances. This freedom in dealing with the Old Testament shows that although the authority of the Old Testament was being maintained in the first century, it was not viewed in a literal sense. Paul is an advocate of a kind of spiritual interpretation of Scripture. He interprets Scripture in light of Christ. Thus when he finds an Old Testament quotation that is useful for his argument, he sometimes alters it in order to make that connection clearer.

The answer to Question 3 of Dimension One shows that Paul has changed the quotation from Isaiah in Romans 2:24. In this instance the Septuagint had already expanded the Hebrew text by adding the phrases "because of you" and "among the Gentiles." In addition to this, Paul has rather drastically altered the original sense of this passage. In Romans 3:4, Paul is much closer to the Septuagint text of Psalm 51:4. From the long series of citations in Romans 3:10-18, I would like to lift up two examples for your group members' attention. The first is 3:10, where Paul has inserted the term *righteous* in order to relate it more closely with his theme that "the righteous will live by faith" (1:17). In the second example, 3:13, Paul uses a fairly literal citation from Psalm 5:9.

The Question-and-Answer Style

Recent advances have been made in our understanding of how Paul's first readers would have perceived the so-called "diatribe" style of 2:17–3:8. Question 2 in Dimension One deals with the "rhetorical questions" that Paul asks at one point that are typical of this style. Previous researchers felt that this was a combative debating style and that the audience was hostile. This view has been overturned by Stanley Kent Stowers in *The Diatribe and Paul's Letter to the Romans* (Scholars' Press, 1981). This professor from Brown University showed that the diatribe was widely used in the public schools of the Greco-Roman world and that its function was to allow the pros and cons about a given subject matter to come to the fore. This style was not used in controversial settings. The audience in this case is perceived to be friendly.

This discovery is significant in view of the long tradition of an anti-Semitic interpretation of these chapters. The fact that Paul is dealing with Jews has often led scholars to think that Paul is criticizing Judaism. But Paul is not dealing with unbelieving Jews at all in this section. He is addressing a friendly audience of the Christian community, which in this instance is made up of Jewish Christians as well as Gentile Christians. They would not have perceived these questions as hostile. Stowers writes, "The dialogical element of the diatribe does grow out of the argument or represents what is typical, but it is directed toward a specific group with which the teacher has a certain relationship. . . . The style is designed for those who have already made the basic commitment" (page 180).

The Issue of Religious Superiority

The major thrust of this passage is that claims of religious superiority must be refuted, no matter what their origin. Whereas the material in our last lesson dealt more directly with Gentile-Christian believers, the material in today's lesson deals with Jewish-Christian believers. The major challenge in presenting this material is to avoid falling into an anti-Semitic interpretation. Many commentaries that you might consult see Paul as arguing against Jews or Judaism in this passage. From the time of the Reformation, indeed nearly from the time when Christianity became the established religion in the Roman Empire, this view has been the major stream of Christian interpretation. The presumed superiority of Christianity over Judaism is seen to be the purpose of Paul's argument. Nothing could be further from the point. This kind of interpretation simply leaves intact the very form of religious superiority that Paul is trying to overcome in Rome.

A major point to be made here is that Paul's targets are Christians and that the argument is a friendly one. Indeed, as we said earlier, Paul goes out of his way in the course of Romans to defend the prerogatives of Jewish Christians. Paul does not wish to attack Jewish culture or the Jewish religion. He wishes rather to make a case for the Roman house churches that the misuse of the great religious heritage of the Hebrew Scriptures is leading to serious disruptions in the life of the community and to the expression of sinful attitudes and acts among the Christian groups. When Paul lists the boasts of the Jews in 2:17-20, he is trying to describe the kind of pride and arrogance that was surfacing in the Jewish-Christian churches in Rome, not to make a general case against the Judaism of his day. The *you* in this argument is clearly the Jewish Christian.

Therefore, when you teach this material, you need to think through ways to relate the Scripture to modern expressions of religious superiority. I think of the feelings of superiority among denominations in the United States, for example. Many denominational conflicts in American history also have witnessed the expression of strong arguments based on the false notion of religious superiority. People having different views of the inspiration of Scripture or different attitudes toward abortion or toward military service, for example, have argued that their religious perception or their interpretation of Scripture is superior. They argue that they are saved and others are damned.

Paul's argument is aimed at overcoming this kind of situation. The argument needs to be recast to make it understandable in the modern world, and this task is one of the most important imaginative chores for the Christian teacher of Romans today.

The Question of Libertinism

In Romans 3:8, Paul deals with a notion that reflects a situation in the early church and in the later history of Christianity. The idea that one might well do evil that good may come, a perverse misunderstanding of Paul's doctrine of salvation by grace alone, is more than a humorous and malicious misstatement. Paul had dealt with a number of instances in the history of early

Christianity when this kind of statement was being lived out. In the Thessalonian church, for example, the sense of membership in the new era and the powerful sense of spiritual change led people to reject the traditional family ethic, to repudiate the heritage of daily labor, and to resist the leadership that Paul had left behind in Thessalonica.

Even more serious were the problems that Paul faced in Corinth. A group of radicals who accepted Paul's doctrine of freedom from the law and spiritual maturity from Christ concluded that all ethics related to the body were now irrelevant. They lived the life of the mind, in their view, free from bodily restraints. In First Corinthians, Paul confronted the excesses of this group. Some of these people preferred sexual union with temple prostitutes to sex within marriage. One person in particular lived in an incestuous relationship. Paul's reference to this in 1 Corinthians 5:1-2 shows that the congregation was actually proud that this person felt free enough in Christ to be able to overcome the repulsion that Greeks would have felt about such a relationship. Many other incidents of this type are found in the Corinthian letters.

Similar examples of lawless and irresponsible behavior have been seen in later Christian tradition. Many times they come from the same kind of feeling of radical freedom and radical change. When one is struck by the force of the gospel, one recognizes the shortcomings of one's former life. One is torn from old loyalties and set free from the moral system connected with one's previous religious heritage. The experience of unconditional acceptance by grace brings a great sense of freedom and exaltation. When the manifestation of the Spirit surfaces, often converted persons have the feeling that they have truly transcended their past and even transcended the world. That one should have to submit to moral limitations and return to an old-fashioned-sounding law seems inappropriate. Furthermore, the freedom of emotions and the high sense of enthusiasm that are often connected with conversion of this sort lead to incredibly warm feelings toward other people, a feeling that sometimes can lead to promiscuity.

Most members of your group will likely identify promiscuous behavior with people who have not been converted. But Paul is dealing here with something that is not at all atypical of people who have undergone a radical conversion experience. Without perhaps consciously living out the logic of Romans 3:8, these persons unconsciously act out this libertinism. This behavior is one of the attendant dangers of a radical kind of Christian faith. In fact, the presence and danger of libertinism is what has led many established church leaders to resist the revivalistic spirit and to question charismatic events in general. Discuss this problem in terms of the experiences of group members. This discussion will help bring the reality of Paul's argument, not only at this point but also in later chapters, into clear focus. Paul is making a case for the kind of transformation that will allow a new and more responsible form of behavior to emerge rather than libertinism.

Works of the Law

Read and discuss Romans 3:20 with the group members. This verse is foundational for the next section of the argument of Romans. Instead of *declared righteous*, use *rightwised*. It is important for the group members to see how this verse relates directly to the thesis of Romans in 1:17.

When Paul refers to "works of the law," he has in mind the kind of works that the Roman house churches were using to prove that each was superior to the others. When people do what the law requires for the wrong reasons, performing acts of mercy and keeping a religious community afloat for the purpose of proving their superiority to others, they fall under the condemnation of this verse.

Paul is dealing here with the most dangerous of Christian vices, self-righteousness. Self-righteousness is the root of Christian arrogance and often is the fundamental cause of conflicts among Christian groups. The problem is that persons and groups use their conformity to a certain standard to try to make themselves "righteous." The whole purpose of Paul's argument from 1:18 on is to prove that this cannot work, that this effort is a form of sinful pride, an effort on the part of creatures to make themselves into the Creator, to gain control of their destiny, and to dominate others.

Paul is forced to make a sweeping and hard case, climaxing in 3:20, because he is confronting the kind of conflicts that will later become characteristic of Christian groups, namely self-righteous groups on the right and left claiming their superiority over others, believing that others are damned or lost. The self-righteous are acting in such a way as to disallow leadership or contributions by others. Paul's hope is to lead the congregation to see that this terrible perversion of the Christian faith is based on the kind of lie to which Romans 1:25 refers. Whereas the Christian groups in Rome feel certain that they are elect and secure, that they are certainly saved, Paul offers a forceful medicine of reality therapy in this argument, ending in 3:20: "No one will be declared righteous [rightwised] in God's sight by the works of the law."

The conclusion of the first phase of Paul's argument, 1:18–3:20, comes in the last two verses. Paul insists that every person loyal to the Hebrew Scriptures must accept the judgment in those Scriptures (3:19). Paul wants to establish a universal kind of accountability. His hope is to lead the Roman house churches to recognize that "no one will be declared righteous [*rightwised*] in God's sight by the works of the law." The thesis that Paul has established in 1:17 comes here to its appropriate development. Until human beings give up the claim that they are righteous in and of themselves and that they are superior to others, they will not be in a position to understand that God's righteousness comes as a gift, that forgiveness is free, and that faith is the basis of a true life.

DIMENSION THREE:
WHAT DOES THE BIBLE MEAN TO ME?

The Issue of Religious Superiority

The issue of religious and cultural superiority is going to make little sense unless it is connected with modern developments. You might think of squabbles among Christians in your local community. You might recollect recent national conventions by major denominations in which conflicts between conservatives and liberals surfaced in prominent ways. You might think of the splits between denominations or between factions in local churches. You might also think of tensions between the major world religions that have surfaced in the Middle East or around the world. An important task is to allow participants' imaginations and their observation of current events to lead them to see that we are all involved in one way or another in the human tendency to make ourselves superior—especially with our religion.

The Issue of Libertinism

The question of thinking through experiences of libertinism is an important one at this stage if the next chapters of Romans are going to make sense. You might think of examples of persons whose powerful religious feelings led them to believe that normal standards of behavior should be abandoned. Bombers or persons involved in crimes for political or religious advantage often perform acts that their religious heritage would not condone. But they do so in the belief that they are loyal to the higher cause, that they will be forgiven, and that grace will cover whatever they do.

No One Has an Advantage Over Anybody

Paul seems to be presenting a paradox when he insists that the Jewish advantage of the law must be maintained while still insisting that all persons, both Jews and Gentiles, have sinned and that no one has an advantage over anybody else. Paul argues this way, not only because of the problems in Rome among the house churches but also because of his understanding of the cross event. That the religious elite of the first century worked with the political leaders to put Jesus to death was a clear indication for Paul of the underlying hostility against God. Paul is inclined to believe that this plight is a universal one. It extends beyond the religious elite of his tradition to every person on earth. So convinced is Paul about this basic revelation of human hostility that he is willing to allow elements of contradiction to enter his argument. He will not give up the other side of the paradox, however, that the Jewish law must be maintained and that the Hebrew Scriptures retain their authority for Christians.

The Issue of Universal Depravity

A major resource for your consideration of this issue might be the work of theologians such as Reinhold Niebuhr, whose great book *The Nature and Destiny of Man* deals with the doctrine of sin. Many other books in more recent times have suggested the psychological and moral significance of this argument. At a time when American culture is having difficulty coming to terms with its own sense of limits and has failed to recognize in any meaningful way the sins that it has committed in its recent history, we recognize the serious social dangers of a society that loses a sense of limits. A doctrine of universal sin helps persons and cultures recognize limits. Until we see the places we have gone wrong, we cannot recognize that we are not superior.

When serious thinkers look about the world, they are sometimes inclined to say that the only Christian doctrine that can be fully proved by objective experience and observation is the doctrine of universal sin. Whatever side the members of your group choose to take on this question, point out the relevance of the issue for the Roman house church situation. Paul can hardly make a case for the Christians in Rome being equal in grace until he can first make a case that they are equal in sin. For, so long as they feel superior and sinless as compared to their competitors, they are unable to grasp the fact that they are all recipients at the same table, sharers of the same unmerited grace. Paul's argument aims at that practical goal.

In this and many other instances keep the same openness with participants that is reflected in the question-and-answer technique Paul uses. Questions and answers allow members of the group to work out their beliefs. This and other teaching techniques will encourage them to come to their own conclusions, to use their own mental energies to evaluate and assess the flow of the argument. Allowing disagreements on crucial issues like this to remain unresolved can be an important step in the direction of recognizing the universality of grace and the pluralism of a genuine Christian community. Everyone does not have to agree with every aspect of Paul's argument in Romans.

It was not through the law that Abraham and his offspring received the promise . . . but through the righteousness that comes by faith (4:13).

FAITH AND ABRAHAM'S CHILDREN

Romans 3:21–4:25

DIMENSION ONE: WHAT DOES THE BIBLE SAY?

Answer these questions by reading Romans 3:21–4:25

1. Assuming that *justify*, *justification*, and *righteousness* are translations of the same Greek term, mark and count the number of times these words are used in 3:21–4:25.

    These words are used twenty times, with at least one instance in which the term is translated two different ways in the same sentence: (1) 3:21; (2) 3:22; (3) 3:24; (4) 3:25; (5 and 6) 3:26; (7) 3:28; (8) 3:30; (9) 4:2; (10) 4:3; (11 and 12) 4:5; (13) 4:6; (14) 4:9; (15 and 16) 4:11; (17) 4:13; (18) 4:22; (19) 4:24; (20) 4:25.

2. Since *faith* and *believe* are translations of the same Greek term, mark and count the number of times these terms are used in 3:21–4:25.

    These two words are used twenty-four times, including two instances in which the term is translated both ways in the same sentence: (1 and 2) 3:22; (3) 3:25; (4) 3:26; (5) 3:27; (6) 3:28; (7 and 8) 3:30; (9) 3:31; (10) 4:3; (11) 4:5; (12) 4:9; (13 and 14) 4:11; (15) 4:12; (16) 4:13; (17) 4:14; (18 and 19) 4:16; (20) 4:17; (21) 4:18; (22) 4:19; (23) 4:20; (24) 4:24.

3. What proportion of the human race does Paul say has sinned? (3:23)

    Paul says that "all [100 percent] have sinned."

4. Does Paul say God belongs more to the Jews or to the Gentiles? (3:29)

    Paul says that God is the God of the Jews and "of Gentiles too."

5. What two important words does Paul retain in quoting Genesis 15:6? (4:3; see also Genesis 15:6)

Paul uses the words believed *and* righteousness *in describing Abraham. The same words are used in Genesis 15:6.*

6. When does Paul say that Abraham received circumcision? (4:9-12)

Abraham received circumcision after his "faith was credited to him as righteousness."

7. Who inherits the promise given to Abraham? (4:16)

Everyone who has faith is an inheritor of Abraham's promise, according to Paul's argument.

8. Mark the verses where the theme of giving life to the dead is developed. (4:17-25)

Paul develops the theme of bringing life from death in 4:17; 4:19; 4:24; and 4:25.

DIMENSION TWO: WHAT DOES THE BIBLE MEAN?

Romans 3:21-28 is the "heart of Romans." In this section Paul makes his marvelous declaration of salvation by faith alone. Here he proclaims freedom from the principle of performance. The righteousness of God in this passage is perceived as God's victory over sin, as shown in the Christ event. This victory transforms humans by making them acceptable to God, despite their failures, despite their rebellion. The setting right of the human race, through the death of Christ, conveys to us the grace of God, which we can never earn. Our lives no longer depend on what we are able to perform, on our obedience to the law. Salvation is understood here as the faithful response of humans to the love of God, as shown in the Christ event.

"Justification by faith" is a matter of being set right by this unconditional love of God, of being restored to the original righteousness that humans were intended to have from the moment of their creation. To stand under this righteousness is to become righteous. "Justification by faith" is also understood by Paul as entering the sphere of divine righteousness, that is, submitting to the lordship of Christ. Thus salvation in this passage is more than feeling accepted. It is a matter of submitting to this righteousness in everyday affairs.

In this lesson we deal with the final two sections of the main proof that supports the thesis in Romans 1:16-17. In 3:21-31, Paul states the positive argument concerning humans being "rightwised" by faith in the one true God. In 4:1-25, Paul sets forth Abraham as the example of such faith and the forebear of all faithful persons. The key term in these final two sections is "rightwising," often translated, as we have discovered, as "justification" or "justify." As the first question in Dimension One has indicated, these terms are used no less than twenty times in 3:21–4:25. Going through these passages and marking these terms will help identify one of the main themes of the section and will review the confusion about how this term should be translated. This reading will also aid the members of your group in seeing the way the material in this section connects with earlier material, particularly with the thesis of 1:17.

The Argument in Romans 3:21–4:25

The abstract quality of Paul's thought in 3:21-31 often leads people to concentrate on individual sentences rather than on the flow of the argument. Perhaps this way of reading is inevitable, but as a group leader you should have a sense of the way the argument as a whole is flowing. In the first phase of the argument, Paul states the major thesis in 21-22a. Verses 22b-26 interpret this thesis, insisting that no distinction can be made between Jews and Gentiles because all have fallen short. Therefore "rightwising" can only be achieved as a gift. This gift is then proved by the citation of a series of traditional confessional statements regarding the significance of Christ and his redeeming act of life and death.

In 3:27-31 the doctrine is discussed with questions and answers. If we can be justified only by faith, then our capacity to boast in our accomplishments under the law is eliminated. Paul restates the reason that this is so by putting forth the idea of "rightwising" by faith alone (3:27).

A second topic concerning the priority of Jews and Gentiles is taken up in 3:29-30, where the oneness of God is related to the doctrine of the justification of Jews and Gentiles by faith alone. In verse 31 a third brief dialogue is begun concerning the status of the law. Several points are stated here that are not fully developed until later chapters of Romans, principally Romans 7.

In Romans 4:1-8, Abraham is shown to be the forebear of the faithful because he was accepted on the basis of his faith rather than on the basis of his accomplishments. In this section the primary and secondary texts are developed that dominate the rest of this chapter. The primary text is Genesis 15:6. The secondary text is Psalm 32:1-2, which indicates that the blessing comes only to sinners, to those who have not worked to accomplish the law.

Romans 4:9-12 makes the point that Abraham's justification occurred prior to the gift of the law and his own circumcision. Paul makes use here of the rabbinic tradition inferred from the Book of Genesis that circumcision occurred several years after Abraham's promise. Faith precedes the law, and circumcision is seen merely as a confirmation of being "rightwised" by faith.

Romans 4:13-25 shows Abraham's promise as having been fulfilled only according to faith. First, Paul makes the point that the promise given to him was not bound by law. Verse 15 suggests that since law provides the basis of measuring guilt, it produces wrath instead of life. Paul goes on in verses 17-22 to show that Abraham, as the ancestor of faithful Gentiles, responded to God and set his faith in the promise given by the one who "gives life to the dead." Since his heir could not have been provided by human means alone, Abraham had to trust in the Creator who brings something out of nothing.

Finally, in 4:23-25, Paul relates the entire argument to the present status of faithful Christians. The promise of being a child of Abraham comes to all faithful persons. The faith of Christians in the resurrected Jesus is therefore the proper fulfillment of the faith in God, who gives life to the dead.

Defining Faith

As your group members will have observed in answering the second question in Dimension One, *faith* is really a crucial term in this passage, being used twenty-four times. It will come as something of a surprise, however, to the members of your group to discover that the Greek term is translated sometimes as "belief" and other times as "faith." The reason for this is that the word *faith* cannot be used as a verb in English. We can speak of *belief* and *believing*, but we do not ordinarily speak of *faith* and *faithing*. The awkwardness of using an expression like "having faith" has led the English translation tradition to separate *faith* from *belief*. The difficulty is that *belief* implies objective dogmas held by the mind. Very often the word *faith* has something of the same content, but in actuality its original significance is that of loyal response to a covenant partner. The analogy of being faithful to one's marriage vows brings us much closer to the biblical content that is needed for this term.

A prominent commentator on Romans defines *faith* this way: "Faith is basically human receptivity, as actively as it may express itself in obedience." *Receptivity* refers to the human response to God's word, which fits very closely into the context of Romans, where the power of the gospel is the guiding theme.

Suggest to the members of your group that they brainstorm on the current meanings of *faith* and *belief*. Discussing these alternatives in an open way will help bring the problem to consciousness and provide resources for the members of your group to distinguish between Paul's view and that of later Christian tradition.

For the sake of understanding what Paul is driving at in Romans, I think we need to abandon the translation of this term as "belief." Paul is referring not to a set of abstract ideas but rather to a relationship. It is the belief side of the Christian faith that was in dispute in Rome and that was leading the house churches to their vicious struggle against one another. Paul is hoping to unify them by offering an approach to faith that is relational. It is a matter of each person setting his or her trust in the Lord, thus submitting to the righteousness of God. I think that the most adequate expression of faith as used in Romans is "loyal response to God's word."

Romans 3:24-25. A number of scholars agree today that the material in these verses did not all originate with Paul. The content of these verses is unparalleled in the Pauline writings. While Paul speaks often, as we have discovered, about grace and "rightwising," he does not otherwise use language such as that found in these verses. The grammatical awkwardness of these verses and the stylistic differences from the rest of Paul's writings have led scholars to suggest that Paul is citing material from early Christian hymns and confessions. The cited material is interspersed with Pauline interpretation.

You might want to underline in your Bible the material that scholars feel is quoted. In that way you can easily identify the material that Paul apparently added. In verse 25, the words "God presented Christ as a sacrifice of atonement, through the shedding of his blood" should be underlined. Also, the words "because in his forbearance he had left the sins committed beforehand unpunished" should be underlined. Some scholars would also add a line from verse 24 to this list of underlined material: "through the redemption that came by Christ Jesus." Although Paul uses the term *redemption* in several other places in his writings, it is certainly not used very often; and this may be an indication that he is citing an early hymn or confession at this point as well.

Many commentaries debate the proper interpretation of these terms and in many instances prefer one over the other. Radical Lutheran theology, for example, sees the language of "rightwising" by faith that Paul integrates into this passage as simply unequal with the Atonement thinking of faith in Christ's blood. Conservative commentators feel more strongly about some of these terms than others, and liberal commentators often redefine terms to make them more palatable. I think it is highly significant, however, that Paul cites these various theories, uses these terms with respect, and is able to integrate them with his own language concerning "rightwising" and faith. A quick look at your text of 3:24-26 shows the degree to which Pauline language has encircled, infused, and incorporated these other materials.

Paul gives no hint of argument here. In contrast to many commentators who feel Paul was "correcting" the more primitive Atonement theories that he cites, it appears to me from the fusion he has created that he has tried to incorporate, authenticate, and validate the theories that were in debate in the house churches in Rome. Paul is making a case in Romans for the coexistence of conservative and liberal branches of early Christianity.

Keep in mind what Paul was trying to accomplish as you present this material to your group members. Be sure to honor the differences in taste and theological perception of the members of your group, some of whom will find more meaning in some of these terms than in others. Perhaps a similar analogy can be found in your preferred hymnal, which probably incorporates hymns from a variety of perspectives into the same collection, thereby honoring a variety of theological attitudes and traditions.

Romans 4:16-25. One of the most striking features of 4:16-25 is the correlation between faith and resurrection. Paul sees the faith of Abraham as faith in God, who can create something out of nothing. Abraham believed that God was capable of creating a son even though Abraham and his wife were far past the age when this was physically possible. God as the Creator is affirmed in the fragment of confessional material that Paul uses in 4:17. The rough transition in verse 17, expressed by the dash in the middle of the verse in the NIV, indicates the use of liturgical or confessional material.

"Calls into being things that were not" (4:17) sounds very much like the Creation theology of Hellenistic Judaism and early Christianity in which God is the one who creates out of nothing. The interest in the question of what was there before Creation and the matter of God creating out of nothing was distinctively Greek. But Paul adapts it here to the Abraham story in a unique way. Abraham's faith is defined as faith in the God who raises the dead. This allows Paul to connect Creation theology with the Christ event, as he does in 4:24-25.

Paul also correlates salvation by faith alone with belief in the Christ event, in particular, belief in the death and resurrection of Christ. Salvation as experienced by early Christians was itself a new creation. It was experienced as the destruction of an old world and the creation of a whole new self. Under grace, persons were able to acknowledge that their former lives had indeed been nothing but that God had been able to create out of that nothing, out of that void of sin and depravity, a new life and a new future. Ernst Kaesemann, in his *Commentary on Romans* (Eerdmans, 1980), makes the clearest sense out of this point:

As hardly anywhere else the full radicalness of Paul's doctrine of justification is brought out here. When the message of this justification is accepted, there is unavoidably linked with it a reduction to nothing which deeply shakes the righteous by associating them with the ungodly (page 123).

The key sentence in 4:25 connects the life, death, and resurrection of Christ and the transformation of humans into the new righteousness. Christ died "for our sins" in the sense that humans discovered their own hostility against God in the death of Jesus. In that death we recognize the depth of human alienation and sin. But we recognize at the same time that we are forgiven at the very moment of Christ's death. He died for the sake of others, guiltlessly, dying in their place so that they might have communicated to them the surpassing grace of God. Since Christ was "raised to life for our justification [rightwising]," Paul is affirming that in the Resurrection the death of Christ was revealed. The theme of dying and rising with Christ, which will be developed in Romans 6, is first expressed here.

Under the power of the Christ event, we recognize that our former lives were null and void and that we have the possibility to share in his resurrection by receiving a new life based on grace rather than on our own accomplishments. For Abraham is indeed the forebear of the faithful of all generations and all times.

DIMENSION THREE: WHAT DOES THE BIBLE MEAN TO ME?

Romans 3:21-31—Experience of Transformation

Since the material in this lesson, particularly 3:21-31, is so widely perceived to be the heart of Romans and therefore most directly related to salvation, participants may have a wide range of experiences to bring to bear on the passage. If you are able to, this would be a good opportunity to talk about their experience of transformation and conversion and their experiences of the lack of satisfaction in life gained from observing "the law that requires works."

Protestants and Roman Catholics on Justification

Christians have struggled for centuries to define what righteousness by faith means. Roman Catholics have consistently maintained that a radical doctrine of justification by faith undercuts the moral transformation required of Christians. Protestants have alleged that Roman Catholic insistence on moral transformation makes up "works righteousness," which is the opposite of genuine faith. A proper understanding of this passage, particularly Romans 3:21-31, would help show the common ground between Protestants and Roman Catholics at this point. It is interesting in this connection that the joint Lutheran-Roman Catholic consultation in 1983 issued an agreement on this point, namely that "salvation rests entirely upon God's merciful action in Christ." The long study released in the fall of 1983 attempts to lay aside the misunderstandings and allegations that have divided Protestants from Roman Catholics on this point for so long.

One aspect of Paul's argument has a particular bearing on this struggle, namely the issue in 3:27 concerning *boasting*. The term relates to the universal human tendency to compete with others and to claim superior status. The problem with the medieval use of indulgences and the system of penitence, Luther charged, was that it encouraged boasting. Boasting is the essence of sin, the reformers taught, because it expresses human rebellion against God. The fall of the human race had consisted in wanting to be like God, capable of boasting; and the essence of false religion, of works, was its boast: "I have performed better than you, therefore I am deserving of God's grace."

The leveling effect of Protestantism is directly related to this insight. If no human should boast of accomplishments, then no one has any claim to be any better than others. All persons are equal before God. Hence the class system is wrong, and every system of privilege should be dismantled. The logic of the radical doctrine of justification by faith inevitably runs toward radical equalization of human honor. Therefore the Protestant impulse is expressed in terms of liberation—of slaves, of industrial workers, of immigrants, of women, of the mentally and physically impaired, and so on and on.

What an irony, however, that this firm grasp of the danger of boasting should have been expressed in ways that led into new forms of boasting. Protestants have boasted that their theology is closer to Paul than that of Roman Catholics. Their boast has included criticisms of Roman Catholics that, in effect, placed Roman Catholics with the Pharisees, outside the Christian faith itself.

Central to Paul's argument is the principle of faith that is stated in 3:28. Here is the formula that marked the most decisive attack on Roman Catholic theology during the Reformation. Some of the confessions of the Protestants included the expression "apart from the works of the law," which became the basis of Protestant orthodoxy. The idea was that humans are acceptable to God solely on the basis of faith, not on the basis of whether they have performed works. The good news in this verse lies at the heart of the Christian faith.

This good news is that no matter how badly we have erred, no matter how far we have fallen from our calling to the disciplined life, no matter how unpopular we are, God loves and accepts us. Nothing we can ever accomplish on our own can provide us this acceptance. One of the thrilling aspects of current church history is that Protestants and Roman Catholics are united in affirming this central point.

The possibility of misunderstanding this gift, however, was there from the beginning; and it has caused suffering, death, and division. The word *faith* tended to be taken by Protestants and Roman Catholics alike as a set of beliefs rather than as a living relationship. Christians tended to infer that if you held a different set of beliefs, you could not gain salvation. For Protestants, "justification by faith" began to be understood as "justification by belief." And a new form of boasting arose: "I am better than you because I have the right beliefs." Roman Catholics, in contrast, held that this kind of radical belief was morally depraved. The boasting of one side came to be counterbalanced by the boasting of the other. In the process the unity of the church was shattered, and the peace of the world was mortally threatened.

One of the features of Paul's argument in Romans 3:21-31 that has been overlooked thus far in the discussion between Protestants and Roman Catholics is that of the oneness of God. The relevance of this idea could hardly be grasped when Protestants and Roman Catholics were so confident that they possessed God in their formulas. I think the psychology of both sides has long led to an unthinking assumption that we have "the one God" on our side. We fight and torture our enemies in the name of that "one God."

Recent advances in our understanding of the Book of Romans make it clear how mistaken this view is. We know that Paul stressed the oneness of God to counter the exclusive claims of first-century liberals and conservatives, comparable to modern Protestants and Roman Catholics in some ways. Halvor Moxnes has made this clear in his study *Theology in Conflict: Studies in Paul's Understanding of God in Romans* (Brill, 1980). Paul's purpose in this section was to address "the problem of divisions between Jews and non-Jews within Christian communities. . . . In this context, 'God is one' served as an argument for the inclusion and co-existence of both Jews and non-Jews in the same community, on the basis of faith" (page 223). Moxnes points out that the argument in these verses concerning the oneness of God as God of the circumcised as well as of the uncircumcised constituted "a conscious effort to include" the less popular Jewish Christians in a hostile Gentile-Christian majority in Rome. The confession that "God is one" was originally meant to unify the Christian community.

When we apply this insight to the long-standing struggle between Protestants and Roman Catholics, we see how dangerous the doctrine of justification by faith was when combined with the belief that God takes sides, that God will oppose any whose definition is different from ours. This makes God into a human possession. It presumes that the God defined in our doctrines is the true and only God. God thus becomes the captive of our theological "work." And this is idolatry. To use Paul's language in this passage, it is a return to "boasting." To claim that God is on our side is this most terrible human mistake of identifying the one true God with our own little causes. In contrast, Paul contends, "God is one."

Just as through the disobedience of the one man the many were made sinners, so also through the obedience of the one man the many will be made righteous (5:19).

GOD'S PEACE AND ADAM'S REALM

Romans 5

DIMENSION ONE:
WHAT DOES THE BIBLE SAY?

Answer these questions by reading Romans 5

1. Which comes first, justification or peace with God? (5:1)
   The gift of justification or righteousness by faith brings with it peace with God.

2. In contrast to the negative view of boasting in Romans 3:27, what are some proper objects of boasting or rejoicing? (5:2, 3, 11)
   Paul describes three things that believers can rejoice in: "the hope of the glory of God" (5:2), sufferings (5:3), and God (5:11).

3. How many times does Paul use the words *righteous, righteousness, justified,* and *justification* (all translated from the same Greek term) in 5:1-21?
   Paul uses these words nine times in Romans 5: (1) 5:1; (2) 5:7; (3) 5:9; (4) 5:16; (5) 5:17; (6 and 7) 5:18; (8) 5:19; (9) 5:21.

4. How is the love of God shown to humans? (5:5, 8)
   God's love is "poured out into our hearts through the Holy Spirit" and shown in Christ's death for sinners.

5. Which experience is reserved for the future—being "reconciled," "saved," or "rightwised/ justified"? (5:9-11)
   "Justified [rightwised] by his blood" is linked with a present-tense verb and thus is portrayed as a current experience for believers. Being "reconciled" is linked with past-tense and present-tense

verbs. Only being "saved" is in the future tense (verses 9 and 10), so being "saved" is an expectation still to come.

6. With whom does Paul say that death originated? (5:12-14)
   Paul says that death came into the world through the sin of Adam.

7. How many comparisons between Adam and Christ does Paul make in 5:15-21?
   Paul makes five distinct comparisons in these verses, each worked out in a different manner: (1) 5:15; (2) 5:16; (3) 5:17; (4) 5:18; (5) 5:19.

DIMENSION TWO: WHAT DOES THE BIBLE MEAN?

The relation of Romans 5 to the rest of the argument of the letter has been clarified in recent decades. Earlier scholars under the impact of the Reformation point of view tended to place this chapter with the first four chapters under the general heading of "justification." One can see the reason for doing this in light of the opening and closing verses of Romans 5, both of which emphasize "rightwising."

A similar kind of division of Romans was popular in nineteenth-century German scholarship, which tended to place Romans 6–8 under the heading of a mystical-ethical doctrine of salvation, while placing 1–5 under the category of a forensic doctrine of salvation. More recent commentators, however, have placed Romans 5 together with 6–8 as is done in this study. Within this framework, Romans 5:1-11 has an introductory role in the series of amplifications of Paul's basic argument that we find in Chapters 5–8. In particular, we see themes in 5:12-21, 6:1-23, and 8:1-39 introduced for the first time in 5:1-11. The restored relationship with God marked by peace provides the basis for future salvation despite all present sufferings. The paradoxical state of the new life is developed throughout Romans 5–8, in that the peaceful relationship with God and fellow humans is set in the context of a world in which the principalities and "powers" are very much present and effective. Christian realism is at the forefront of this passage.

The Artistic Structure of Romans 5:1-11

The role of this passage as a kind of hinge between the first and second sections of the formal argument of Romans is enhanced by the structure that Paul provides. The people in the Greco-Roman world were much more sensitive than we are to the way an argument is structured. They took particular delight in *chiastic* patterns in which the themes of an argument are crossed and reproduced in reverse order. We find a clear chiastic structure between the opening and closing verses of 5:1-11. In the first three verses the theme of "peace with God" is followed by the theme of rejoicing in hope and affliction. These themes reappear in reverse order in 5:11, which opens with rejoicing in God and closes on the theme of peace in the form of "reconciliation." The ancient audience of Romans would have felt at verse 11 a satisfying sense that the section had been rounded off and completed in an artful manner.

The "Eschatological Reservation"

At several points in Romans 5, we encounter what scholars of a previous generation called the "eschatological reservation or proviso," an insistence that the final form of Christian fulfillment will take place only at the end of time. We find this proviso for the first time in 5:2, in which "the hope of the glory of God" is placed in the context of future hope rather than present experience. Even more clearly we see this in verses 9 and 10, where "rightwising" and reconciliation are contrasted with the future salvation. We see the same kind of contrast in 5:17 and 6:8.

Likely, Paul makes this distinction in order to insert a note of realism into early Christian enthusiasts. These persons believed that, with the dawn of the new era and the gift of the Spirit, they were already participating in the resurrected life. This belief implied that troubles would be completely eliminated and that evil had been overcome. Paul's contention in Chapters 5–8 is that the Christian life must be lived out against the threats of a still-fallen world. He does not wish to deny that regeneration has already occurred and that the new life is presently available. What the "reservation" implies, however, is that the fulfillment is yet to come. The Christian life makes no sense in the context of troubles and afflictions without the principle of hope. Any Christian who loses sight of this will remain terribly vulnerable in times of persecution and natural disaster. The peace that we have with God sustains us through persecution and trouble; it does not relieve us from them.

The Puzzle of Romans 5:12

This verse contains one of Paul's incomplete sentences, which mark particularly difficult and paradoxical parts of his argument. The incomplete quality of his sentence is somewhat disguised by modern translations that fail to provide a capital letter for the first word of verse 13, which would indicate that it is indeed a separate and independent sentence.

Verse 12 begins as the first half of an elaborate comparison, but the comparison is never completed. The first sections of this sentence present a thoroughly deterministic view of sin and death as caused by the first humans, Adam and Eve. But in light of the earlier argument in Romans, Paul is not content with this traditional and despairing determinism. Having argued so vigorously in 1:18–2:29 for free responsibility, Paul wishes to insist upon it here as well. Thus the final three words of verse 12 state the other half of the paradox: "because all sinned." It has been suggested that the paradox itself caused Paul's sentence to break off in midstream. Regardless, the incompleteness of this sentence marks a significant issue within Pauline theology, an issue that participants may wish to discuss in some detail.

An important question is whether Paul advocates the traditional Christian doctrine of "original sin," which Augustine stated so eloquently much later in Christian history. Augustine's theory and the one accepted by Roman Catholic theology through most of Christian history is that the sin of the first humans was related to sexual desire. Original sin in this sense is carried forward by the sex act itself so that each person born from human sexuality carries the infection of human sin. This doctrine sustains the high value placed on the virgin birth and the immaculate conception of the virgin Mary in modern Roman Catholic dogma. It is also related to the ideal of a celibate priesthood.

Paul's writings give no hint that he interpreted sin as related to human sexuality. In fact, he had a more positive attitude toward the human body than much of Western Christianity has had. Therefore we should more appropriately describe Paul's view as that of "universal sin." He was convinced, in light of the Christ event, that all humans are involved in rebellion against God and that everyone stands in need of forgiveness. In 5:12-21 he develops the idea that Adam, as the first human, brought such sin into the world and became an effective power for subsequent world history. This view was widely shared in first-century Judaism. But Paul is unwilling to follow this determinist line through to the end. He wishes at the same time to maintain that each human is responsible for his or her own sin. Hence the addition of the paradoxical line in 5:12 concerning all humans sinning of their own free will.

The content of verse 12 gives you an opportunity to let participants voice various attitudes toward sin and the universality of evil. Some members will likely have a much stronger affinity for the final three words of 5:12 than for the preceding theme of the universality of sin after Adam. Either side of this paradox has strong Christian support. That sin is universally binding seems to be confirmed by observing the human scene. Yet if we take this idea alone, it can undercut individual responsibility for sin. Ethics and the law require individual accountability that the social causation theories of sin in their modern forms tend to undermine.

The strength of the voluntaristic view of sin is that it stresses human accountability. Its weakness is that it often is connected with an overly rosy appraisal of human perfectibility. And this view finds it difficult to account for the social poison that seems to influence the great bulk of persons in negative directions. Perhaps a serious discussion of this age-old problem in your group will increase appreciation for Paul's somewhat illogical and paradoxical solution. It is more than mere inconsistency. Paul, in light of the Christ event and loyal to his biblical tradition, wishes to affirm both the universality of sin and human accountability.

The Identity of "The One to Come"

Most commentators have assumed that the "one to come" in verse 14 refers to Christ and that Paul is preparing for the contrast between Adam and Christ in the next verses. This identification causes problems, however, because Paul does not really argue that Adam and Christ are similar. Those who hold this view are forced to build more contrast into this verse than Paul actually states.

Another approach may be suggested if members of your group raise this question, and that approach is to identify the "coming one" with Moses, who is also mentioned in verse 14. The contrast between Adam and Moses is basic to this sentence, and in a very real sense Adam prefigures Moses because both stood in Jewish theology in clear relationship to the law. The main

GENESIS to REVELATION **ROMANS**

point of verse 14 is that sin is intrinsically related to death, a point that Paul made with other argumentative means in Romans 1. In the Genesis story death was perceived to have come with Adam, but death also marks the rest of the history of Israel and the present time as well. Paul believes that this reign of death also pertains "over those who did not sin by breaking a command, as did Adam"; that is, persons who allow other forms of sin and rebellion are likewise under the power of death. From this wording we see that Paul is not advocating the idea that everyone exactly model his or her behavior after that of Adam. The element of free will, which we noted at the end of verse 12, manifests itself here as well.

The Image of Adam in Ancient Judaism

The members of your group may be interested in gaining a fuller picture of the way the figure of Adam was understood in the Judaism of Paul's time. A double interest surfaces in the literature of the intertestamental period and of early Judaism. On the one hand, Adam is the one who originated sin for the human race and caused death to reign. On the other hand, he is the one who had a true relationship with God, bearing God's image.

The idea of Adam as originating death, causing the corruption of human life, and beginning the era of sin that sweeps over all humankind is widely affirmed in the Jewish tradition. One writer speaks of Adam as the one on whom the commandment was placed; "but he transgressed it, and immediately you [God] appointed death for him and for his descendants" (4 Ezra 3:7). That humans were immortal before the Fall is also widely assumed. One writer says that "from a woman sin had its beginning / and because of her we all die" (Sirach 25:24). That the flood of evils afflicting humankind derives from Adam is also widely affirmed. Disease, mental anxiety, and murder and other moral sins are all seen as caused by the inaugurating sin of Adam.

Other writings of Judaism, however, affirm very strongly human responsibility for sin in a way that is quite similar to Paul. Second Baruch 54:15-16, 19 states the following: "For, although Adam sinned first and has brought death upon all who were not in his time, yet each of them who has been born from him has prepared for himself the coming torment. And further, each of them has chosen for himself the coming glory. . . . Adam is, therefore, not the cause, except only for himself, but each of us has become our own Adam."

The image of the exalted Adam also is quite widely shared in ancient Judaism so that there was substantial basis for understanding Christ as a kind of second Adam. The idea that Adam was the image of the humanity God intended in creation, a humanity that would be restored at the end of time, began to arise. When this occurred, of course, the role of Adam as the bringer of death and the originator of human sin tended to be downplayed. Several writers, in fact, suggested other explanations, blaming the Fall on Eve or Satan or the fallen angels. Sometimes Adam is shown as the first king, and in other instances the glory of Adam is emphasized. One writer refers to Adam as a creature "honorable, great, and glorious" (2 Enoch 30:11). I have found many affirmations of the idea that with the coming of the kingdom of God, true believers will regain the glory that Adam lost. Later rabbinic writers made a great deal of the glory of Adam and the wisdom that he showed. Prominent also was the idea of the gigantic body of Adam in which God created each subsequent person on earth.

Compared with these traditions, it is striking how sober and limited the role of Adam is in Romans 5. Paul uses Adam to contrast the world of sin with the world of salvation. Paul apparently wished to make plain that every person has to choose between Adam and Christ. To fall back into pride, arrogance, and self-will is to fall under the power of death once again. This choice had a direct bearing on the Roman house churches, which needed to understand the depth of sinfulness that was manifesting itself in their behavior. The promise of abundant grace and the "gift of righteousness" (5:17) needed to be cherished and lived out.

In a sense each Christian needs to recognize that the "old Adam" threatens to surface. The promise of the new life is heightened by its contrast to the old. As Robin Scroggs writes in *The Last Adam* (Fortress Press, 1966), "In order to speak of death Paul has to refer to Adam's sin; yet his major goal is to show that what lies ahead for the believer is the restoration of life, the life which had been God's intent for Adam. It is no accident that the section ends in verse 21 with an exultant affirmation of the gift of eternal life through Christ" (page 82).

DIMENSION THREE: WHAT DOES THE BIBLE MEAN TO ME?

The questions raised in the participant book for this lesson point to personal experience in a large way. In order to make the abstract but powerful argument in Romans 5 understandable, it needs to be brought into relation to everyday experience. The critical judgment of the members of the group is also required at a number of points. In addition to this, two types of resources are suggested to bring out the meaning of this text.

The Relevance of African American Spirituals

The sense of experiencing faith in the midst of a world of affliction and suffering is supremely embodied in the traditional African American spirituals. The remarkable sense of rejoicing in our sufferings (5:3) is found in the well-known song "Nobody Knows the Trouble I See." This spiritual conveys the strong sense of identification with Jesus, who shares our troubles and bears our sins (5:8). Because of the certainty of the presence of God's love and the experience of it in the worship service (5:5), we have the possibility of rejoicing in the midst of suffering. The theme of this song is very close to the theme of Romans 5.

The significance of hope in the experience of suffering is also particularly prominent in the African American spirituals. Without such hope, affliction becomes impossible to bear. It destroys one's humanity.

The search for a firm relationship that will sustain one through suffering reflects the concern for "perseverance" and "character" referred to in Romans 5:4. The result of such a profound relationship with God as portrayed in the African American spirituals is peace:

> I've got peace like a river,
> I've got peace like a river,
> I've got peace like a river in my soul.

This sense of life as a constant struggle, of the tension between a firm relationship with God and the current conditions of slavery and injustice, comes very close to the sense of the overlapping ages that we found in 5:12-21. The realm of Adam with its trouble and sin is consistently contrasted with the realm of Christ and the true homeland of believers. This sense of moving between two ages is particularly prominent in many of the spirituals. The unfriendly world of suffering leads the singers of the African American spirituals to be firmly convinced of their true homeland with Jesus.

A Separate Peace

Among the pieces of American literature that deal with the themes in Romans 5, I think particularly of John Knowles's novel *A Separate Peace* (Macmillan, 1959). This novel deals with the yearning to discover a private Eden where the evil of the world is overcome. The shock at the center of this novel is that evil rears its head even in the peaceful realm of "a separate peace."

The story tells of a group of students in a private Eastern school during the Second World War. The narrator, Gene, makes the discovery of the truth of Romans 5:12, so to speak, that all persons are involved in evil. When he is talking to his good friend Finny in the hospital room just before the operation that proves fatal, Gene tries to explain why he had jounced the limb to throw his friend out of the tree: "It was just some ignorance inside me, some crazy thing inside me, something blind, that's all it was" (page 174).

Whatever this thing was inside Gene, the novel reveals that he had desperately tried to conceal its incriminating presence. One of his friends penetrated this disguise: "You were always a lord of the manor, weren't you? A swell guy, except when the chips were down. You always were a savage underneath. I always knew that only I never admitted it" (page 128).

In the course of the novel, Gene comes to acknowledge this academic savagery within himself. And he uses this self-discovery to make sense out of the baffling world in which he lives. He uses it to explain the war: "Wars were not made by generations and their special stupidities, but . . . were made instead by something ignorant in the human heart" (page 183). When persons and nations find themselves pitted against evil in the world around them, they respond savagely and reach out to destroy and to cripple.

This point is worth reflecting on because Knowles here presents an explanation for war that is much closer to Paul's letter to the Romans than to the generally accepted view in our culture. Our assumption has typically been that war is caused by evil aggression on the part of enemies. Good persons and the good nation, though they may have minor flaws, are never pictured as the cause of the violent conflict. But Knowles has the audacity to shatter this stereotype, presenting savagery as an integral part of life. Gene, the most brilliant student in the class, is a savage underneath.

The novel *A Separate Peace* also deals with the sense of collective responsibility for sin that Paul describes with the Adam motif. Gene discovers that all relationships at Devon Academy are based on enmity, that a kind of savagery is carried out in the sports and even in the friendships in the school. This savagery is also connected in some way with the atmosphere of fear that pervades Devon. Gene notes it as he revisits the campus at the beginning of the novel, recognizing this atmosphere more clearly now that he has escaped from it. He sees now that when he used to walk up the long white marble flight of stairs, "specters seemed to go up and down them with me" (page 3). This savagery is also connected in some way with the rules, with what Paul calls in Romans 5:20 the law that came "so that the trespass might increase." The message in the Devon chapel services was that if you broke the rules, they would break you. The guilty obsession with the rules is expressed at many points in the novel.

In contrast to the other characters in the novel, Finny alone is perceived to be somehow free from the compulsion about the rules. His vibrant sense of life simply overcomes these petty boundaries. He skips class at the slightest pretext and breaks the dress code with such disarming innocence that he invariably gets away with it. This peculiar freedom from the law is also connected with the seeming sense in which Finny alone is free of the savagery that marks everyone else in the novel. His philosophy, for example, is that everyone wins in sports, that they are not a savage contest: "Finny never permitted himself to realize that when you won they lost. That would have destroyed the perfect beauty which was sport. Nothing bad ever happened in sports; they were the absolute good" (page 26).

Phineas (Finny) alone seems to escape the universal plight described in Romans 5:12. "He possessed an extra vigor, a heightened confidence in himself, a serene capacity for affection which saved him" (page 184). The author pictures this young man as a person who retains his childhood innocence because of his self-confidence and affection. And this lack of savage rivalry is the essence of his inner peace. "Phineas was the essence of this careless peace" (page 16) that marks the summer session at Devon that is remembered in the novel.

The belief that someone, somewhere escapes the universal dilemma of savagery therefore lies at the center of the appeal of this novel. Yet John Knowles does not allow this optimistic picture to remain intact. He ends up close to Paul in Romans. Finny is shown toward the end of the novel as refusing to accept the reality of evil in himself or in his friends. He steadfastly refuses to accept the fact that Gene really had jounced the tree and that behind this action was, in Gene's words, "a primitive impulse to kill." When Gene reveals that he had done it, Finny responds with uncharacteristic vehemence: "I'll kill you if you don't shut up." Gene answers him, "You see! Kill me! Now you know what it is! I did it because I felt like that!" (page 59). When the investigation into the cause of the accident reveals beyond a shadow of a doubt that Gene, in fact, had done it, Finny must flee this recognition and tumbles down the marble stairs, in effect, ending his own life. The best the doctors can do cannot preserve him.

In a real sense the tragic ending of this novel rests in the refusal to recognize what Paul argues, that "death reigned from the time of Adam." To deny our limitations and to deny that there is savagery even in the best of us is to refuse to recognize our humanity. To believe this is to render oneself incapable of facing life in the real world. Sin becomes even more inevitable for those who deny it. There is no separate peace, no insulated refuge on this earth. The only peace that is available to us occurs in the midst of a fallen and broken world in which savagery remains.

Now that you have been set free from sin and have become slaves of God, the benefit you reap leads to holiness, and the result is eternal life (6:22).

SET FREE FROM SIN

Romans 6

DIMENSION ONE:
WHAT DOES THE BIBLE SAY?

Answer these questions by reading Romans 6

1. What does Paul say about the idea of remaining in sin "so that grace may increase"? (6:1-2)
   Paul says, "By no means!"

2. With which does Paul connect baptism, with Jesus' life or with Jesus' death? (6:3-4)
   Paul connects baptism with Jesus' death.

3. What is the outcome of Christ's resurrection? (6:5)
   The outcome is that Christians "will . . . be united with him in a resurrection like his."

4. Is the sharing of Christ's resurrected life a present or a future prospect? (6:5, 8)
   Since Paul uses future-tense verbs, "we will certainly also be united with him in a resurrection like his" and "we will also live with him," sharing Christ's resurrected life is solely a future prospect.

5. What is the result of being crucified with Christ? (6:6)
   The result of being crucified with Christ is the destruction of "the body ruled by sin" so that "we should no longer be slaves to sin."

6. To what does Paul suggest that the parts of your body should be offered? (6:13, 19)
   Paul suggests that "every part" of the body is capable of being "offer[ed]" to God "as an instrument of righteousness."

7. What does Paul say about the possibility of being a "slave"? (6:16-18)
   Paul argues that everyone is a slave "of the one you obey," whether it be sin or obedience.

8. What was the "benefit" of being a slave to sin? (6:20-23)
   The "benefit" or "wages" of sin is death, according to 6:21 and 6:23.

9. How many times are the words *life, alive,* and *live* used in 6:1-23?
   Paul uses these terms a total of twelve times: (1) 6:2; (2 and 3) 6:4; (4) 6:8; (5, 6, and 7) 6:10; (8) 6:11; (9) 6:13; (10) 6:19; (11) 6:22; (12) 6:23.

DIMENSION TWO: WHAT DOES THE BIBLE MEAN?

In Romans 6, Paul continues to deal with the implications and objections of his doctrine of the righteousness of God. In 6:1 he takes up the issue that arose from the last verses of Chapter 5, that grace abounds more than the increase of sin. Verse 2 addresses this issue by pointing out the inconsistency of living in the realm of sin. Verses 3-7 explain this principle of inconsistency, showing that in baptism, believers have experienced the death of Christ and are set free to live in a new life with Christ. As your group members have discovered from answering Question 9 in Dimension One, the theme of life runs through Romans 6, with a particular emphasis on living as agents of divine righteousness. The conclusion of the first section of the argument in verse 14 states the proper relation of grace to law by maintaining that sin cannot reign over those in Christ.

In Romans 6:15-23, Paul raises the rhetorical question that arose from the final verse of the preceding section. If believers are "not under the law, but under grace," is there any necessity for moral urgency? Paul answers this question in the negative on the basis of the idea of the exchange of lordship, first stated in verse 16. Salvation here is understood as being redeemed from an old lord and made the slave of another. Romans 6:17-20 provides an expansion of this basic idea, contrasting the new lordship with the old. Romans 6:20-23 lifts up the consequences of the two lordships, the one leading to shame and death and the other leading to holiness and life.

Baptism With Christ

One of the major lines of interpretation of Romans 6 deals with the sacramental aspect of Paul's thought. Roman Catholic scholars were particularly interested in baptism as an experience of sacramental union in which saving grace is communicated and a new life is begun. Some scholars who are particularly oriented to the Greco-Roman religious scene have suggested that Paul was modeling his theology at this point on the mystery religions. In some of these Greco-Roman cults, initiates underwent a ceremony of dying and rising with the cult god or goddess. The result of such a ceremony was regeneration and the gift of divine power. Just as the god or goddess demonstrated divinity by triumphing over death, so the initiate was presumably given a form of immortality by going through the ceremony.

As can well be imagined, these suggestions for interpreting Romans 6 have raised a storm of protest and criticism. In particular some Protestant theologians and Bible scholars have been critical of the sacramental interpretation of Romans 6. One of the results of this discussion is the recognition that the Pauline language does not provide a precise analogy between the rite of going down into the water and coming back out in baptism on the one hand and the death and resurrection of Christ on the other. Jesus did not die by drowning. And there is no attempt in Paul's description of the baptismal experience in 6:3-4 to copy Jesus' crucifixion. Even more difficult, however, is that Paul refrains from completing the parallel of rising out of water and rising from the dead. Nowhere in this passage does the Christian gain, in this experience of baptism, present access to a resurrected state. Instead, in 6:4 Paul shifts into the metaphor of living a new life; and in verse 5 the participation in Christ's resurrection is separated from the baptismal event and postponed until the end of time.

So we cannot argue for a complete correspondence between the ritual of baptism and either the death and resurrection of Jesus on the one hand or an alleged death and resurrection of Christians on the other. One of the most striking aspects of Paul's use of the baptismal metaphor is what one writer has called the "element of temporal extension" in which the moment of baptism is seen to lead toward a life that is lived out toward the future triumph of righteousness with the return of Christ. The framework for Romans 6 is not so much the baptismal ceremony itself but rather the death of Christ and the return of Christ.

The Problem of Christ-Mysticism

The references in this passage to living with Christ and being identified with his life and death have led some scholars to suggest that a fundamentally mystical concept of the faith is being presented here. The references to the identification between the believer and Christ, according to this interpretation, come not from baptismal experience but from the charismatic and mystical experiences in which the Spirit joins the believer with God.

One of the best-known studies along this line is Albert Schweitzer's *The Mysticism of Paul the Apostle* (Holt, 1931). He suggests that the center of Paul's theology is the idea of bodily union, not only with each other but also with Christ, a union that in a particular way "manifests the power of the death and resurrection, thereby achieving the status of resurrection before the general resurrection has occurred" (page 116, my translation from the German original).

Schweitzer argues that Paul believed in a kind of double resurrection, that as Christ has a resurrected body, so the believers possess a resurrection body by virtue of their entrance into the messianic community in baptism. Phrases such as *in Christ, in the spirit,* and *Christ in us* should be interpreted on the basis of this bodily existence, capable of current resurrection, shared by the individual Christian in Christ. To sin after baptism is thus a fundamental violation of this new life, a sign that the power of the Resurrection has not yet taken effect.

This provocative hypothesis explains much about Pauline thought. But it does not do justice to Romans 6, in which Paul so clearly and explicitly reserves the believers' participation in the resurrection to the future (6:5, 8). In fact, in Paul's authentic letters he always sets the resurrection in the future. (See Philippians 3:10, 21.) In contrast, the so-called Deutero-Pauline epistles (those letters whose authorship has not positively been credited to Paul) indicate the possibility of current participation in the resurrected state (Colossians 2:12; Ephesians 5:14).

Much of Schweitzer's interpretation, however, remains valid even when corrections are made. You will perhaps observe in the commentaries that you consult how hostile a reception Schweitzer's book had and how much suspicion remains in scholarly circles against any idea of Pauline mysticism. The reason for this view is the long tradition of the Reformation, in which Martin Luther had difficulty with Christian mystics and enthusiasts.

We cannot deny that in Romans 6 substantial elements of mysticism are present. Paul does have a kind of personal relationship with Christ that is intense and real. This relationship is seen in Paul's intense prayer life and his expectation that the life of the believer should pattern itself after the life of Christ (6:10-11). But keep in mind that the kind of physical mysticism that is indisputably part of the Pauline tradition is also a kind of historical mysticism. Paul places the believer in the context between the death and resurrection of Christ, which is a past event, and the resurrection, which is a future event.

Those who wish to grasp the distinctive contours of Pauline mysticism, therefore, must take pains to separate it from traditional mysticism. Normally in a mystical theology, one is joined with the divine force so that a kind of union is achieved. This union sometimes involves even a loss of personal identity as the person is absorbed into the divine realm. A second distinctive feature of traditional mysticism is the loss of temporality. One has the sense in mystical experience of being set free from time, of being reunited with past or future figures and events. Time in such an experience seems to stand still or to be irrelevant. One has the sense of participating in divine time or in timelessness.

In both these regards Pauline mysticism is very different. Rather than a fusion between the believer and Christ, there is rather a kind of marriage, a relationship in which Christ remains Lord and in which the believer remains the servant. Romans 6 anchors the believer securely in this world between the poles of the death and resurrection of Christ in the past and the future resurrection and the triumph of righteousness at the end of time. The frequent shifts between present, past, and future verbs make this anchoring in time a distinctive and unusual feature of Pauline mysticism.

We also find little of the expected kind of inactive contemplation in Pauline mysticism. The result of baptism when properly understood is that Christians view themselves as "instruments of righteousness" (6:13) whose task is to yield themselves "as slaves to righteousness leading to holiness" (6:19). The ethical dimension of the Christian life is completely fused with Pauline mysticism in these verses.

The Idea of a "Change of Lordship"

An aspect of Romans 6:15-23 that may be a particular problem for your group members is the stress on being "slaves." We find this in verse 16, where Paul makes it clear that humans do not have a choice of being slaves; the only question is whom they serve. This point is a problem in a culture whose primary moral category is "freedom."

The assumption of American culture that there is such a thing as absolute freedom runs flatly counter to Romans 6. Paul's argument in 6:16 rests on foundations he laid down earlier in this letter, namely that human beings are natural idolaters. Humans cannot live without gods, without idols; so when humans refuse to recognize and worship the true God, they set about to create their own (1:23). Paul believes that humans are incapable of pure and absolute freedom. They wish to subordinate themselves to something, to serve something larger than themselves. They feel too puny to stand alone. When we think we are serving ourselves, in fact, we are serving some cultural image or idol, some image of what we believe we ought to be.

Salvation, therefore, appears to be a matter of exchanging lords, of shifting from an evil master to the proper and true master. Ernst Kaesemann has made popular the idea of salvation as "a change of lordship." He writes concerning Romans 6:16,

> It is presupposed here as elsewhere that a person belongs constitutively to a world and lies under lordship. With baptism a change of lordship has been effected. . . . The new [lord] sets those who are bound to him into freedom from powers and necessities. . . . We receive our freedom in allegiance to him and as a result of the right of lordship which God has graciously established over us. . . . He who belongs to the true cosmocrator [lord of the universe] strides erect through his sphere of power, breaks all the barriers and taboos arbitrarily set up there, and thus walks no less confidently through the sphere of the Torah, bearing witness thereby, in spite of appearances to the contrary, to God's peace on the earthly battlefield and to openness for brethren as the truth of the reign of God and as an announcement of the world of the resurrection (*Commentary on Romans*, page 179).

We can see from this formulation that Kaesemann does not wish to understand the lordship of Christ as resulting in a kind of Christian servility. We will follow this theme as it develops in Romans 8.

The Issue of Sanctification

When Paul mentions *holiness* (sanctification) in 6:19, he is stating an issue that is fundamental for this chapter. For centuries Protestants have tended to separate justification and sanctification. They viewed justification as the beginning of the Christian life and sanctification as verifying it.

One result of this distinction is that sanctification is viewed as secondary, as a kind of add-on to the Christian life. A related problem is that justification was seen as the result of grace much more than sanctification was. The door was left open for sanctification to be seen as a human effort to conform oneself to the new law of God. Since this view so easily resulted in a new and devastating form of legalism, some Protestant thinkers downplayed sanctification and denied that it was possible or even feasible. Salvation was thus defined in Protestant orthodoxy as having the proper belief, while the issue of proper behavior was relegated to the secondary realm.

John Wesley made a major contribution at this point. While he sometimes followed the traditional separation between justification and sanctification, he insisted that sanctification was an expectation for all Christians. He wrote the following summary of the main points in "A Plain Account of Christian Perfection":

(1.) There is such a thing as perfection; for it is again and again mentioned in Scripture.

(2.) It is not so early as justification; for justified persons are to "go on unto perfection." . . .

(3.) It is not so late as death; for St. Paul speaks of living men that were perfect. . . .

(4.) It is not absolute. Absolute perfection belongs not to man, nor to angels, but to God alone.

(5.) It does not make a man infallible: None is infallible, while he remains in the body (*The Works of John Wesley*; Zondervan, n.d.; Vol. 11, pages 441-42).

Some features of Paul's argument in Romans 6 counter some of the negative tendencies of the traditional approach toward sanctification. One of them is that Paul understands sanctification as the natural result of the shift of lordship. Holiness is not understood as a merely human activity, the result of humans following high ideals. In 6:19, Paul refers to us offering ourselves "as slaves to righteousness leading to holiness [sanctification]." Here the "rightwising" activity of God is understood to be united with the sanctifying activity of God, and both come to those who submit themselves to the gospel.

The union between justification and sanctification is even more firmly secured by our current understanding of justification as "rightwising," in which the righteous control of God over the entire world is in prospect. That humans could be "rightwised" without having their lives altered is inconceivable for Paul. This helps us understand the central thrust of Romans 6, that Christians cannot content themselves with a life under sin after they have been made part of the new era.

Sanctification for Paul is therefore not a human achievement. It is the gift that comes from a new relationship with God. Sanctification is closely related to the task of Christian believers to "offer every part of yourself to [God] as an instrument of righteousness" (6:13). Paul would therefore find completely unnatural the currently popular division between evangelism and social action. For him, response to the gospel implies that one becomes a member of the realm of righteousness and promotes righteousness in everyday life as an automatic consequence. Sanctification must be united with justification if Romans 6 is to be properly understood.

The Problem of Interpreting Body In Romans 6

At two points in Romans 6 the term *body* is used in a peculiar way. In 6:6, Paul refers to the "body ruled by sin" being "done away with" or rendered powerless, which could lead us to think that a kind of physical death was required of the physical body in order for sin actually to be overcome. The tradition of the "mortification of the flesh" has strong support in the wording of this verse. Paul's use at this point sounds very close to gnostic dualism, with its negative view of the body and its belief that salvation was strictly a matter of the mind. Also peculiar, though in a different way, is Paul's expression in 6:12 concerning not allowing sin to reign "in your mortal [dying] body." Why Paul stressed mortality in this particular verse needs an explanation.

Some scholars have held that the expression "body ruled by sin" or "body of sin" (6:6) referred to the mass of sins that one had committed in one's former life or was perhaps a figurative expression for the body of sinful desires. These interpretations try rather unsuccessfully to avoid the inference that this idea of the destruction of the sinful body would bring Paul close to gnosticism. The problem is not just that this reference implies that sin roots in the physical substance of the body but also that redemption would appear to take place by means of the destruction of the body.

That such ideas were current in the Pauline communities is shown by the reference (NIV, 1984) in 1 Corinthians 13:3, "If I . . . surrender my body to the flames, but have not love, I gain nothing." These facts make it hard to avoid the conclusion that Paul in 6:6 has likely taken over a gnostic expression of some kind that was being used in the early church. But he corrects this understanding by inserting the decisive words *of sin*. These words not only serve to exclude the idea that the person who has transcended bodily existence was free to sin but also shift the blame of the human dilemma from the physical body to sin as a power in the old age. The expression "body ruled by sin" is therefore likely the result of Paul's correction of the gnostic understanding of baptism as providing a destruction of the body.

Whereas a reference to the "dead body" would be quite appropriate in 6:12, expressing the idea that in baptism we die with Christ, I find it difficult to explain why Paul in fact uses the formula "mortal body" in this verse. One theory suggests that Paul was countering the libertinistic assumption that since the body was mortal, it was morally indifferent and could not affect the spiritual center of the person. This suggestion could be correlated with the observation that scholars have made, namely that Paul in Romans 6 refers to death with Christ in the past tense but to resurrection with Christ in the future (6:5, 8). That Paul is trying to correct the overly intense enthusiasm of some Christians at this point is widely assumed.

The use of the term *mortal* in 6:12 may well be part of an effort on Paul's part to correct an overly enthusiastic belief in the present possession of immortal life. By insisting on the continued presence of the mortal body, Paul seeks to avert the false conclusion that some people might have drawn from his references to having already died with Christ. He therefore guards against the danger of believing that death for the believer is a thing of the past.

DIMENSION THREE:
WHAT DOES THE BIBLE MEAN TO ME?

Be Free

To grasp the shape of Paul's idea of change of lordship in Romans 6, some comparisons with current culture might help. Ask if some members of your group remember the lyrics of any popular songs that express the yearning to "be free." Write these lyrics on a whiteboard, a chalkboard, or a large piece of paper and compare them with Paul's view. Since group members may prefer Paul to the composers of contemporary songs—especially while they are in the class setting—use care to make fair comparisons.

Yielding to Righteousness for Sanctification

When discussing Romans 6:19 in relation to John Wesley's view, it is interesting to recall that Wesley claimed that his views were entirely scriptural and had not essentially changed since early in his ministry. Albert C. Outler pointed out the originality of Wesley's view and said that

> Wesley asserted that his doctrine of "Christian perfection" had been the creative focus of his understanding of the Christian life from his first conversion to "serious" religion in 1725, and that it had continued as such without substantial alteration. He was as vitally concerned with the "*fullness* of faith" (i.e., sanctification) as with its beginnings (i.e., justification); as confident in the *goal* of the Christian life as of its *foundation*. He tried earnestly to maintain the parallelism between justification and sanctification—both by faith!—and between those good works appropriate to the reconciled sinner and to the mature Christian as well. This insistent correlation between the genesis of faith and its fullness marks off Wesley's most original contribution to Protestant theology (Albert C. Outler, ed., *John Wesley*; Oxford University Press, 1964; page 251).

Ask participants to think about what it would take for them to commit to and work toward Christian perfection. Remember that this does not mean sinlessness, but rather having one's heart, head, motivations, and actions completely aligned with the will of God.

The Old Age and the New Era

The idea of the Christian life poised between the old age and the new era has often been described as like standing between the invasion of Normandy by the Allies in June of 1944 and the climax of VE day, when victory in Europe was proclaimed. The beachhead of Jesus Christ's life signed the death warrant for the realm of sin and death, but fierce battles had to be fought before the terrain could be reconquered. Without the certain hope of a future triumph, those involved might not have had sufficient courage to continue.

We have been released from the law so that we serve in the new way of the Spirit, and not in the old way of the written code (7:6).

 9

SET FREE FROM THE LAW
Romans 7

DIMENSION ONE:
WHAT DOES THE BIBLE SAY?

Answer these questions by reading Romans 7

1. How many times is the word *law* used in this passage?

    Law is used twenty-three times in this chapter: (1 and 2) 7:1; (3 and 4) 7:2; (5) 7:3; (6) 7:4; (7) 7:5; (8) 7:6; (9, 10, and 11) 7:7; (12) 7:8; (13) 7:9; (14) 7:12; (15) 7:14; (16) 7:16; (17) 7:21; (18) 7:22; (19, 20, and 21) 7:23; (22 and 23) 7:25.

2. When is a woman considered free from the law of marriage? (7:1-3)

    A woman is free from the law of marriage when her husband dies.

3. What things are "aroused by the law," leading to death? (7:5)

    "The sinful passions" are "aroused by the law" and work toward our death.

4. Does Paul say that "law" or "sin" is responsible for leading people to break the commandments and to fall into death? (7:7-14)

    Paul argues that "sin" is responsible for death (7:9), whereas the "law is holy . . . [and] spiritual" (7:12, 14).

5. What causes Paul to do, as he confesses, "what I hate"? (7:15, 17, 20)

    Paul argues that "sin living in me" causes him to do what he does not really want to do.

6. What is Paul's attitude toward the law? (7:22, 25)

Paul "delight[s] in" and is "a slave to God's law" in his "mind," while with his sinful nature he serves the law of sin.

DIMENSION TWO: WHAT DOES THE BIBLE MEAN?

The argument in Romans 7 can be conveniently divided into three parts. Romans 7:1-6 describes life in Christ as freedom from the law. This section takes up the theme of the law that was announced in 6:14. The idea of a change of lordship or jurisdiction that we picked up in Romans 6 is stated in the form of this rhetorical question in 7:1. Romans 7:2-3 develops the analogy of secular marriage law to establish the point that jurisdiction does not continue after death has occurred. Verses 4-6 then apply this principle to Christians who died to the law in experiencing this shift in lordship through Christ. Under Christ, a new relationship in the Spirit is established.

The second section, Romans 7:7-12, answers an objection concerning the law that arises out of Paul's statement in 7:5. His reference there to the sinful passions being aroused by the law could easily lead to the objection that law now falls into the moral status of sin. This false conclusion Paul denies in 7:7 and then goes on to explain with the idea that the law makes humans conscious of sin. Romans 7:8-11 elaborates this idea, showing that sin merely found an "opportunity" in the law, leading to covetousness and death. This section is concluded by verse 12 reaffirming the point that the law is holy and good.

The third section, Romans 7:13-25, answers an objection that could arise from Paul's references to the deceit of the law in 7:11 and the goodness of the law in 7:12. The question in 7:13 deals with the effect of the law on humans. Paul's thesis is that sin invaded the law to produce death. This thesis is sustained by the argument in 7:14-23, showing how sin prevents a person from achieving the desired good. This is followed by the statements of 7:24-25 about the wretchedness of the human plight and the blessedness of the grace of God, who saves humans from this plight through Christ. The final half of verse 25 summarizes the argument.

Romans 7:1-6. Here Paul develops a comparison between marriage law and the situation of Christians standing between the two ages. The point of the comparison, as is easy to discern, is that once the husband dies, the woman is free from the marriage contract. Paul argues in the conclusion of this argument (7:4-6) that the law has jurisdiction only in the old age and that those who belong to the new are comparable to the woman whose husband has died. She is free and so are those who had formerly been held under bondage to the law. The reference to being "in the realm of the flesh" in 7:5 refers to the status of persons in the old age, shaped by self-seeking and the kind of sinful self-will that is characteristic of Paul's use of *the sinful nature* or *the flesh* in a context like this.

This question of freedom from the law as a mark of the new era plays a role in the conflict that has been discerned between the weak and the strong in Rome. In all probability, the conservatives were arguing that the Jewish law continues its jurisdiction in the new era. The thrust of Paul's argument at this point is clearly on the side favored by the strong, namely that with the dawn of the new era, the law no longer has jurisdiction. But it is interesting to observe that at the end of 7:6, Paul makes it clear that members in the new era continue to "serve," not in the old way, bound by the law, but in the new ethical situation of being bound to Christ. The crucial question for Paul is whom does one serve?

Romans 7:7-12. An interesting point is that the only commandment mentioned in 7:7-12 is the one concerning coveting. Paul follows a Hebrew tradition at this point that suggests that coveting was the beginning of all sin. The desire to assert oneself against God and the neighbor is revealed in coveting what the neighbor has and refusing to accept what in faith should have been viewed as the gift that God has given each person uniquely. This commandment stands close to the word *desire*, which is used in Paul's earlier argument in Romans, translated as "shameful lusts" (1:26).

Robin Scroggs has developed this theme of covetousness as the essence of sin in his book *Paul for a New Day* (Fortress Press, 1977). He connects covetousness to aggression and to Paul's basic idea that "sinful existence is *hostile* toward God." Scroggs suggests that

> covetousness is a primary expression of aggression—the attempt to possess, control, seize from another, and, metaphorically at least, to kill. To be obedient to the Torah in an attempt to justify oneself by works covertly expresses that primal hostility and aggression against God the Father. Aggression is the reaction against the authoritative, awesome Father, who says, "Thou shalt not . . . ," thus putting an end to freedom. The obvious act of rebellion is, of course, to defy the commandment (pages 12-13).

Scroggs goes on to suggest that a substantial element of rebellion and submissiveness is found in all obedience and that the sense of manipulating God by the law is closely associated with the idea of covetousness. Scroggs points out that Paul's expression "every kind of coveting" (7:8) points to this wide-ranging effort by humans to base their lives on their own achievement under the law. Scroggs writes, "Life under law is a life of *total covetousness*. And covetousness is death" (page 11). Scroggs explains this connection by a theory of Oedipal energy in which the yearning to possess results in aggressive feelings toward parents. Submission to the law can become simply a form of this hostility. Whether this Freudian explanation is on track or not, Paul's own personal experience of persecuting the church suggests the serious effects of what Paul called our "shameful lusts."

Romans 7:13-24. A set of terms surfaces at the end of Romans 7 to explain how humans come under bondage to the law. An expression in this connection is 7:14, translated in the NIV as "I am unspiritual, sold as a slave to sin." The word *unspiritual* actually translates the word *fleshly*, a term that then connects directly with Paul's statement in 7:18 that "good itself does not dwell in me, that is, in my sinful nature (flesh)." Paul then moves to the cry of the captive, "Who will rescue me from this body that is subject to death?" (7:24). The two major lines of interpretation that have been used in the past to understand Paul's references to *sinful nature* (flesh) and *body* in Romans 7 are both in need of substantial revision. A brief description of these alternatives will help lift up the issues that need to be dealt with concerning Romans 7.

The idea of flesh and body as signs of human sensuality was widespread in earlier phases of Pauline research. This tradition was heavily influenced by the Greek heritage, which pitted the "lower nature" against the "higher nature" of the mind and spirit. This dualistic interpretation of Paul assumes that Paul had a negative view of the human body and in particular a negative view of human sexuality. This concept of flesh as sensuality surfaces in the medieval Roman Catholic idea of renunciation of the flesh as a means of holiness. It also surfaces in various forms of Puritanism and Protestant moralism in which the body is viewed as the source of temptations and evil.

The study of Paul's letters to the Corinthians is primarily what led scholars to revise or reject this traditional view. In 1 Corinthians 6:12-20, for example, Paul lays out a positive theory of sexual relations and contends that "the body . . . is . . . for the Lord, and the Lord for the body" (1 Corinthians 6:13). His comment later in this section that "your bodies are temples of the Holy Spirit" (1 Corinthians 6:19) would be impossible for anyone holding a dualistic viewpoint. Also, Paul's positive view of marriage in 1 Corinthians 7 makes it clear that Paul rejected the dualism that was so characteristic of his society. Scholars who have attempted to understand Pauline theology on the basis of Jewish foundations have been particularly sensitive at this point. In contrast to the Greco-Roman world, the Jewish culture had a generally positive appraisal of the body and of the created order. To make Paul into an advocate of sin as sensuality is to bring his theology all too close to gnosticism.

A second and more widespread misinterpretation of Paul's concept of flesh and body concentrates on the issue of weakness. In this line, *flesh* symbolizes the inability of persons to achieve high ideals. This view was also popular in Puritan and post-Puritan thinkers. Whenever we are told that we know what is right but we do not have the willpower to do what is right, we are following this line of interpretation from Romans 7. This view has expressed itself in two different theories about Paul. The first is the idea of the weakness of the Jews to obey the law. This idea was followed by Martin Luther and in general by the liberal theologians of more recent times who adhered to that tradition. This interpretation, as we have shown above, is a complete misinterpretation of first-century Judaism. And it imposes on Paul a kind of introspective conscience that was not characteristic of him.

A second way to apply this interpretation is to stress the weakness of Christians to obey the law of Christ. This interpretation leads to the conclusion that every Christian must recognize the impossibility of perfection in this life.

The major problem with this interpretation is that it runs so strongly counter to the argument that Paul has developed in Romans 6. Paul himself gives no indication that he found it impossible to live out the Christian ethic. He exhorts his fellow Christians not to let sin "reign in your mortal body. . . . But rather offer yourselves to God as those who have been brought from death to life; and offer every part of yourself to him as an instrument of righteousness. For sin shall no longer be your master" (6:12-14).

In addition to flying against the clear implications of Paul's argument in Romans, this interpretation also has some negative effects on the shaping of the Christian self-identity. It leads people to a sense of self-pity and an expectation of failure. The resultant stress on the lack of determination and willpower tends to lead people back into a form of works-righteousness that is completely resistant to grace.

And as for those who succeed in fulfilling the Christian obligations, this interpretation lures them into an overly boastful attitude concerning their superiority over others. A self-image that fluctuates wildly between guilt feelings and insufferable superiority is one of the results of this misinterpretation of Romans 7.

The third alternative, which is advocated in this Bible study, suggests that Paul is showing the dilemma of the self-righteous person in Romans 7. He is describing his own experience as a persecutor of the church, zealously convinced that his own view is correct and therefore running pell-mell into opposition against God.

The dilemma of Romans 7 is seen to be explicitly laid out in Romans 10:1-4. In that latter section, Paul refers to Jews who "are zealous for God, but their zeal is not based on knowledge." Paul goes on to say, "Since they did not know the righteousness of God and sought to establish their own, they did not submit to God's righteousness." These verses accurately describe Paul's own situation before his conversion. His life was not marked by a lack of zeal or a lack of righteousness, understood as conformity to the law. The basic flaw was the failure to recognize that God was revealed in a new and revolutionary way in Christ. The failure to submit to the righteousness of God meant that something profoundly wrong lay at the heart of that piety that had marked Paul's earlier life. Rather than weakness of will or the lure of his sensual desires, Paul's problem was his zealous commitment itself. Only in the light of the cross event, as confirmed by the Resurrection, did Paul discover that his righteousness had a terrible internal flaw. The very good he sought to achieve, namely to obey God's will, turned against him; and he found himself an enemy of God.

This interpretation of Romans 7 potentially has wide relevance in understanding the circumstances of our current world. And it also allows us to understand the evidence within the Pauline letters in a straightforward way.

The consequence is that when Paul uses *flesh*, he is talking about the unconsciously self-centered, self-justifying tendency of humans. The person who is "unspiritual [fleshly], sold as a slave to sin" (7:14), is being held in bondage by this covetous orientation to the law. So long as the real motivation of the self is to gain justification, to prove superiority over others, this element of unconscious sin has corrupted the goodness of the law. Thus when Paul refers to deliverance from "this body that is subject to death" (7:24), he is describing the body dominated by the law of sin. The problem of humankind resides not in our physical bodies but rather in the sinful distortion of human desires that turns even the goodness of religion into its very opposite.

Romans 7:25. Romans 7:25 alludes to the resolution of the problem described in Romans 7. This line picks up the themes that we have studied, particularly from Romans 3:21–4:25; 6. Paul is convinced that the grace of God as revealed in the Christ event finally exposes the self-righteousness of humans. In killing the Christ, the pious community was holding to its own righteousness. In zealously conforming to its law, religious persons found themselves opposing the righteousness of God. But Paul also discovered in the Christ event the possibility of forgiveness. When persons are struck by grace, their former efforts to gain status through conformity to the law drop aside as unnecessary. The illusion that humans can produce the perfect good by themselves drops away, and they begin to recognize themselves as they really are—finite creatures whose best glory always falls short of the glory of God. But they are also creatures loved by God, unconditionally. A new basis for self-esteem is thus offered and a new kind of work begins to emerge—work not aimed at boasting, but rather responding to the boundless grace of God.

The gospel thus provides a deliverance from the plight described in Romans 7. The argument in Romans 7 had a direct bearing on the Roman house churches that were responding to their threatening circumstances by discriminating against others and by trying to prove their superiority to others. Paul shows, through this argument in Romans 7, that such behavior is simply a sign of returning to the old age of bondage to the law. Any good that one achieves through such methods will turn out to be evil. Only by understanding our lives as based solely on grace do we have a possibility of overcoming the power of this covetousness in which *I* oppose the status that others have because *I* want the central status for myself and my group alone. Thus when Paul says at the end of the chapter that "in my sinful nature [flesh] [I am] a slave to the law of sin," he is describing the actual motivational structure of the house churches at Rome, locked in their battle with one another. Such battle is the flat repudiation of genuine faith.

DIMENSION THREE: WHAT DOES THE BIBLE MEAN TO ME?

Legalism

Since Americans are no longer shaped by the same kinds of legalism that marked an earlier generation or even the time of Paul, we need to consider whether Paul's argument has a direct bearing anymore. I believe that a good case can be made that the modern consumer society offers a similar appeal to "the flesh."

You might organize an experiment to test Paul's argument, making use of advertisements from television, magazines, or newspapers. In particular, I am thinking of the kind of advertisements that offer something beyond the product itself as a result of buying it. If one buys the "right" toothpaste or automobile, one wins the affection of the lovely or handsome partner. If one drinks the "right" beer, one gains fellowship and fulfillment. The motivation in these ads is to conform to the law in the sense of buying a particular product with the promise that fullness of life will be achieved.

Use the collection of ads to discuss the theme of covetousness, which is central for Romans 7. Some of the ads in some "upper class" magazines have this element of covetousness combined with high levels of hostility. One ad, for example, once advertised an automobile so rare and expensive that your neighbors could not buy one even if they wanted one. The caption on the ad was, "Demoralize Thy Neighbor." The idea of gaining a particular product that will lend prestige and permanent superiority is a characteristic new form of the law that, if Paul is right, leads to death rather than to life.

The theme of the flesh and sinful passions aroused by the law is illustrated by many of these ads. An advertisement can arouse the desire to gain a particular product so that by having it one will have achieved life. The "sinful passion" that leads buyers to follow the logic of such an ad is the yearning to gain something by one's own effort that secures life and renders one secure from vulnerability and criticism. But a disappointment pattern follows the law just as surely as is described in Romans 7. The good that one hopes to achieve fails to arrive. Thinking through the logic of the ad and the likelihood that one's love affair will really be guaranteed by the toothpaste or that one's marriage will be secured by the automobile allows one to gain a modern-day conception of Paul's basic point: "What I want to do I do not do, but what I hate I do."

It is entirely possible that participants are not sucked in by such ads, but analyzing what they offer, and purport to offer, may yield fruitful discussion of what values are stated and implied, and how group members do buy in in other ways.

Conflicts Between Children and Parents

The internal contradiction of a zealous attachment to the law that ends up in its opposite could be reconstructed from news accounts of conflicts between children and parents. In a typical account that was published several years ago, a young man fell increasingly out of communication with his parents at the age of fifteen. His father was a salesman and active in the Little League and the Boy Scouts. The father became increasingly critical of the lifestyle his son was adopting. His son was attracted by the drug scene and often came home high.

The father and son came to blows several times as the father tried to force the young man to conform. He only wanted the best for this boy, but things continued to get worse. At one point the father placed a tap on the family telephone to check up on the boy—a ploy that backfired and increased the hostility. In one flare-up he told his son the following:

> I've tried everything I know to do. I've tried to reason with you, I have forbidden you to see kids who take drugs, I have asked you to stay home, I've taken you to family court, I've cried, I've told you I loved you, I've told you I'll do anything in my power to find you help. Your mother and I cannot talk to you anymore. So this is the way it's going to be. You're going to stay home Friday and Saturday nights if I have to lock you in your room.

After the young man wrecked the family car while driving under the influence of drugs, the fatal encounter took place in the ranch-style home in the suburban development. The boy demanded to know whether the father had reported his use of drugs. When no answer was forthcoming, the young man started after his father with a steak knife. The father pulled the trigger on the police revolver that he had in his belt. The bullet tore directly into the young man's heart, and he was dead.

The father had sought the good for his son, but it turned out to be evil. "I do not understand what I do. For what I want to do I do not do, but what I hate I do."

Hopefully, this example is far more drastic than the experience of group members, but it can be used to start a conversation about the lengths to which people go to try to love and support, as well as to defy.

We know that in all things God works for the good of those who love him, who have been called according to his purpose (8:28).

10
NEW LIFE IN THE SPIRIT
Romans 8

DIMENSION ONE:
WHAT DOES THE BIBLE SAY?

Answer these questions by reading Romans 8

1. How many times are the words *Spirit* and *spirit* used in 8:1-27?

> *The words* Spirit *and* spirit *are used twenty-two times in these verses: (1) 8:2; (2) 8:4; (3 and 4) 8:5; (5) 8:6; (6, 7, and 8) 8:9; (9) 8:10; (10 and 11) 8:11; (12) 8:13; (13) 8:14; (14 and 15) 8:15; (16 and 17) 8:16; (18) 8:23; (19 and 20) 8:26; (21 and 22) 8:27.*

2. What are the marks of the "minds set on what the flesh desires"? (8:5-8)

> *Paul associates the "minds set on what the flesh desires" with death (8:6), hostility to God (8:7), a refusal to submit to God's law (8:7), and an inability to please God (8:8).*

3. What does Paul say about those who do not have the Spirit of Christ? (8:9)

> *Paul says that "if anyone does not have the Spirit of Christ, they do not belong to Christ."*

4. What does the Spirit communicate to believers who cry, "*Abba*, Father"? (8:15-17)

> *The Spirit confirms that we are children of God and co-heirs with Christ.*

5. What does Paul say the creation is expecting? (8:19-21)?

> *Paul says the creation longs (a) "for the children of God to be revealed" (8:19), (b) to "be liberated from its bondage to decay" (8:21), and (c) for "the freedom and glory of the children of God" (8:21).*

6. How does Paul describe the Christian hope? (8:24-25)

Paul writes that "we hope for what we do not yet have."

7. What is the role of the Spirit? (8:26-27)

The Spirit "helps us in our weakness" and "intercedes for us."

8. List the verbs used in 8:29-30 to describe God's saving activity.

These verbs describe God's saving activity: predestined, called, justified (rightwised), and glorified.

9. How many experiences and powers does Paul list in 8:35-39 that cannot "separate us from the love of God that is in Christ Jesus our Lord"? What are they?

If one lists the final, cumulative item of "anything else" in 8:39, Paul lists seventeen experiences and powers in these verses: (1) trouble, (2) hardship, (3) persecution, (4) famine, (5) nakedness, (6) danger, (7) sword, (8) death, (9) life, (10) angels, (11) demons, (12) the present, (13) the future, (14) powers, (15) height, (16) depth, and (17) anything else in all creation.

DIMENSION TWO: WHAT DOES THE BIBLE MEAN?

In Romans 8 we turn to some of the most relevant and accessible material in Paul's letter. You will perhaps find that for many members of your group this is the chapter of Romans they find most intriguing and most directly significant for daily life.

This chapter is divided into three large portions. Verses 1-17 deal with the cosmic struggle between the sinful nature (flesh) and spirit. In this section the work of the Spirit is integrated with the concept of salvation by portraying the Spirit as it conveys unconditional acceptance (therefore "rightwising") to believers. The second section, verses 18-30, deals with the hopeful suffering of the children of God. This section discusses the cosmic context of Christian faith. The third section, verses 31-39, provides a conclusion for not only Romans 8 but also for all the material from Romans 5:1 onward. Its theme is that nothing can separate believers from the love of Christ.

We begin our consideration by studying the various approaches to the flesh/spirit tension in Romans 8. This material has been very influential in Western culture, primarily in a way that reflected some serious misunderstandings. The idea during the monastic period that true Christians should renounce the sinful nature rests on this passage. The ideas during the Puritan period of renouncing worldly honors and in the later Victorian period of renouncing sexual pleasure are both directly related to the idea of the minds set on the spirit versus the minds set on the sinful nature (flesh). These ideas also have had a direct impact in the most important American forms of entertainment, as will be discussed in the final section of this lesson.

Romans 8:1-17. In the first two questions in Dimension One, our attention is drawn not only to the centrality of the spirit but also to the marks of what Paul calls the "minds set on what the flesh desires" (8:6-8). The elaborate description of the differences between the flesh and spirit has been subject to a variety of interpretations throughout Christian history. The classic position developed by Eastern Orthodoxy was that Paul was a Platonic thinker and that this tension between flesh and spirit was between the sensual nature of humans and the pure realm of divine reality. This interpretation viewed evil as coming from the material realm and resulted in a grave suspicion of the body and of human sexuality. The spirit, on the other hand, was viewed as the realm of pure ideas, untouched by history or materiality. This approach to Paul is far too dualistic. It places flesh and body in too thoroughly negative a context and overlooks the central notion of sin that was laid down in Romans 6 and 7 as a foundation for what Paul is arguing in this passage.

The approach to the flesh/spirit dualism in Western Christianity was decisively shaped by Augustine. He offered a modified form of biblical Platonism. For him, flesh equals human nature in its conscious revolt against God. The lust of humans to gain life on their own accord is particularly associated by him with the sexual drive. But it is also rooted in human weakness. In contrast, spirit is understood as the divine will that sets moral limits to humans. This approach comes much closer to the Pauline view in Romans 8, but it still identifies flesh too closely with human sexuality. This approach also does not reflect very clearly the tension between the two ages reflected in this passage.

The view of the flesh/spirit dualism that emerged in the liberal theology of the nineteenth and twentieth centuries tended to view flesh as self-righteousness or human weakness. The inability of humans to perform the high ideals and to live up to the law was identified as the major problem of humankind. *Spirit* in this tradition tended to be viewed, not as the vital miracle-working action of God, but rather as the collection of high ideals toward which humans should strive. The high ideals of the "brotherhood of man and the fatherhood of God" tended to be set against the fleshly side of humans, consisting of the reluctance to live up to expectations.

Breaking off from the liberal view, the perspective of the Christian existentialists was that flesh equals human dependency on self. *Spirit* in the interpretation that grew in the 1920s to 1960s was viewed as the manifestation of the Christ event whose subjective side was the knowledge that persons had of the Christ event, a knowledge that provided a new self-understanding. The existentialists tended to view the flesh versus the spirit dualism as a tension within the human psyche alone. The historical tension that is particularly evident toward the end of Romans 8 was completely lost from sight.

The most important steps in the direction of the view presented in this study were taken by two German scholars, Werner Georg Kuemmel and Ernst Kaesemann. Both scholars pointed out the cosmic dualism that is implicit in Paul's perspective. Both took account of the wording of Romans 8:7 concerning the sinful mind that is "hostile to God." That flesh acts independent of

GENESIS to REVELATION **ROMANS**

humans and is something of a power sphere was suggested by Kuemmel but finally and clearly developed by Kaesemann. In his more mature work Kaesemann identifies flesh with the old age and believes that people are thoroughly determined by the world to which they give their loyalty. Spirit, therefore, designates the new era and flesh the old. When Paul speaks of the sinful mind (flesh), he has in mind the world view around us and the powers that dominate our current society. They exercise an attraction for humans in particular directions, which, as Paul has shown in the earlier argument of Romans, are directly related to the social consequences of Adam's sin.

In the work that I have done on this problem (*Paul's Anthropological Terms*; Brill, 1971), a case was made that Paul's use of *flesh* arose directly out of the Judaizer crisis in the late AD 40s. *Flesh* came to designate the circumcised flesh of people who were advocating circumcision as necessary for salvation. It also came to be identified by Paul as the cosmic power of the old age, the age of self-justification and sin. We find this idea reflected in Romans 8. *Flesh* in Romans is characterized by the sinful desire to gain righteousness by works. Such a life leads to death because in depending on our own flesh to gain righteousness, we come into conflict with the righteousness revealed in the new era. The power of the flesh was broken by Christ, who came in the flesh. Henceforth life may be achieved through obedience to the law by means of the spirit, and in this way the bondage to the flesh is superseded by life according to the spirit.

In Romans 8, Paul uses *spirit* as the apportioned spirit passed out to humans, as we can see in verse 15 as well as in verse 10. The Spirit is also identified with Christ and is perceived to be the mark of the new era, manifesting itself in charismatic forms as well as in transformed ethical behavior. Therefore the kind of dualism that Paul has in mind in Romans 8 is between the two ages, the new era of Christ and the old era of Adam. Paul's contention in this chapter is that these two ages are in opposition to each other and that, when Christians find themselves living "according to the flesh," they are really falling back into the old age. Whether they intend it or not, the consequence is to come into opposition to God (8:7-8).

Liberation by Christ

A key term in Romans 8 is that we are "set . . . free from the law of sin and death" by Christ (8:2). This theme is dominant for the entire section, and it is developed in detail as Paul describes the work of Christ setting humans free from "the flesh." By sending Christ "in the likeness of sinful flesh," Paul suggests that God "condemned sin in the flesh" (8:3).

As we have seen from earlier chapters of Romans, Paul believes that the Christ event reveals the depth of human hostility against God. The function of Christ is to expose evil but also to relieve humans from it. That is why Paul urges that the consequence of salvation is to walk "according to the Spirit" (8:4). This verse develops the key theme of Romans 6, that those who belong to the new era become "slaves to righteousness." The means by which this transformation occurs, according to 8:3, is the sending of the Son in the "likeness of sinful flesh." By this Paul means that Christ was similar to us, yet not identical at the point of sharing the rebellion of humans, which is the essence of human sin. Christ shared our humanity but not our revolt. By exposing human self-righteousness and alienation, Christ set humans free from their bondage.

The death of Christ is understood in Romans 8, as elsewhere in Romans, to be the exposure of human sin, its condemnation, and its overcoming by pure grace. It results in a transformation of life so that the law is actually accomplished. What God wills for humans, namely that they accomplish the good, is made possible when the human rebellion is ended. Grace overcomes the hostility that had distorted the human race, a point that links Romans 1:18-32 with the striking words of Romans 8:7: "The mind governed by the flesh is hostile to God; it does not submit to God's law."

Romans 8:5-7. In 8:5-7, Paul describes the two realms of the sinful nature (flesh) and the spirit in constant opposition to each other. "The power sphere that attracts your loyalty determines your perspective" is the point set forth in 8:5. When Paul describes this outlook in terms of hostility and resistance to the law of God, he has in mind his own previous experience, as we saw in our interpretation of Romans 7 in the last lesson. Paul's persecution of the church for not conforming to his own standards and his resistance against Christ as a lawbreaker were revealed to him on the Damascus road as signs of an unacknowledged hostility against God. Here in Romans 8, Paul explains the kind of paralysis of the will that was described in Romans 7:19: "For I do not do the good I want to do, but the evil I do not want to do—this I keep on doing." When Paul adds to this the idea that the sinful mind "does not submit to God's law," he has in mind the aggressive misuse of the law as a means of status formation. It is not that Paul or other Jews of his time were unable to obey the law. Far from it. The problem, as Paul discovered in his conversion, was that his perfect obedience to the law had unconsciously become a means of zealous rebellion against God.

Paul's point in this section is that the aggressive, competitive outlook of humans is determined by the old age. This outlook is built into human institutions and cultural systems. That is why Paul believes that "flesh" is more than simply a human individual characteristic. It has to do with what we would call today "the social world." This kind of behavior pattern, "the mind governed by the flesh," is pitted against a completely different outlook that Paul believes ought to be characteristic of the Christian community. The "mind governed by the Spirit" is one that is capable of recognizing limitations. It is cooperative and therefore gives evidence of having overcome hostility and class differences.

Paul's idea of two mindsets and two power spheres in combat with each other had great relevance for the Roman house church situation. In a sense Paul is suggesting that the situation in Rome indicates that the "mind governed by the flesh" was still dominant there. What was needed in Rome were the features that Paul particularly identifies with the "mind governed by the Spirit," "life and peace" (8:6). *Life* is understood to be an orientation toward realistic and mature relationships. It is full of thankfulness, but it is willing to accept death. Life in this sense is correlated later in the chapter with future hope and resilience in the face of opposition. The word *peace* in 8:6 has to do with overcoming barriers and hostility. It is a noncompetitive outlook. Peace involves harmony, not only with fellow humans but also with the world around us. Harmony was clearly a key issue for the Roman house churches. By contrast, the "mind governed by the flesh" is oriented, perhaps unconsciously, to competition and death. It is hostile, which results in separation between humans and God as well as between humans themselves.

Romans 8:12-17. The function of the Spirit to convey a sense of acceptance and self-identity is stressed in 8:12-17. That Christians are "led by the Spirit of God" (8:14) was widely assumed in the Roman house churches. But Paul connects this acceptance in a profound way to the main thesis of his letter, the triumph of divine righteousness and the conveyance of unconditional acceptance. To be given the Spirit according to 8:14 means to be confirmed as "children of God." This idea is elaborated in terms of the strong feeling of acceptance and belongingness that is far from the spirit that "make[s] you slaves" in 8:15.

Paul goes on to connect this spirit of "sonship" with a term that the early church picked up from the historical Jesus. In a unique way, Jesus referred to God as "Abba," an intimate address to God, which might be translated "Papa" or "Daddy." Since this was a foreign word for Paul's Greek audience, he translates it here with *Father*. Jesus used this term for God to show the intimate sense of acceptance that he felt. Thus Paul suggests that when Christians find it possible to speak to God on terms as intimate as they would use with a parent, the Spirit is conveying to them that they are "God's children."

Paul refers to our crying out this acclamation. The ecstatic element of early Christian worship and devotional life is in view here; and quite likely the term *Abba* was closely related to glossolalia, or speaking in tongues. This means that the experience of the Spirit does not make Christians divine. Rather, when properly understood, it conveys to us that we are unconditionally loved by the Abba. We are truly "God's children," beloved and accepted. As children, we are no longer outsiders; we are no longer slaves and subordinates. We are honored members of the household of God and inheritors of the promises.

Romans 8:18-30. The context for the struggle between the two ages, as Paul describes it in Romans 8, is far more than personal. It is cosmic. The struggle involves the whole creation, which is consistent with the thesis of Romans concerning the righteousness of God, because, as we saw earlier, *righteousness* has to do with God's righteous control over the whole created order.

Humans in relation to their environment are directly involved in what Paul has in mind. As we can see in 8:18-25, humans are intimately related to their environment. The world itself has suffered from human sin and arrogance. When referring to the creation being "subjected to frustration" (8:20), Paul probably had in mind the Hebrew conception that sin corrupts the world. Today we understand this idea in terms of the distortion of ecology, the destruction of war, the exploitation of nature by human greed and arrogance. Paul refers at this point to the theme that was characteristic of the Hebrew interpretation of the garden of Eden story. Human sin is seen to corrupt even the soil itself (Genesis 3:17-19).

That the creation therefore "waits in eager expectation for the children of God to be revealed" (8:19) has to do with the expected transformation of humans in their relation to their environment. So long as humans remain bound by sin, the earth continues to suffer. Only when the human race is transformed will the ecology of this planet find its order once again. Paul refers in 8:21 to the hope of creation being "liberated from its bondage to decay" and obtaining "the freedom and glory of the children of God." This means that the creation itself will be restored to its original righteousness and beauty as humans are restored. In the meanwhile, as Paul describes it in 8:22, the whole creation along with us is "groaning as in the pains of childbirth."

The result of this cosmic view is that salvation for Paul requires an element of hope. This hope is defined by the thesis of Romans, the recovery of the righteousness of God, which involves God's control and restoration of the whole created order. The hope here is not for individual salvation alone but also for the salvation of the planet. The emphasis on hope makes it plain that Paul does not believe that Christians living in the Spirit are already beyond their status as mortal human beings. Christians, as well as their environment, are still subject to the long legacy of the "mind governed by the flesh."

The distortion of human life, the erosion of the environment, and even the threat of death as a result of human sin are all implicit in this view. For Paul, the life of faith is lived between the ages. Death and disease are still a reality for Christians and for others. The hope that keeps us going is anchored in the triumph of divine righteousness at the end of time. Christians "wait for it patiently" (8:25) because they are certain that the triumph of Christ will come at the end of time. The daily struggle that Christians carry out is a struggle in behalf of this goal. Here we see what Paul had in mind in Romans 6 when he referred to believers becoming "instruments of righteousness" (6:13).

Romans 8:26-27. At two points in Romans 8, Paul uses language reminiscent of the ecstatic elements of Christian worship. The most explicit of these is 8:26-27, where the Spirit is described as helping humans in their weakness by "wordless groans." Ernst Kaesemann in particular has made the case that Paul refers here in a positive way to early Christian glossolalia, the phenomenon of speaking in tongues. In the Pauline churches, speaking in tongues was understood to be inarticulate speech, the sighing and groaning of the creature at a level far too deep for human articulation. Kaesemann detects a polemical element, however, in the context in which Paul places this reference to speaking in tongues. Since it was understood to be heavenly speech in the Pauline churches and since enthusiasts in places like Corinth took great pride in their ability to speak in tongues, Kaesemann finds it striking that Paul places it here in the context of "weakness":

> Heavenly speech can be heard in worship as a work of the Spirit. But what enthusiasts regard as proof of their glorification [Paul] sees as a sign of a lack. Praying in tongues reveals, not the power and wealth of the Christian community, but its [weakness]. The Spirit . . . has to intervene if our prayers are to have a content which is pleasing to God. He does so in such a way that even in worship he brings us to that groaning of which the unredeemed creation is full and which speaks out of the longing of the assaulted for the redemption of the body (*Commentary on Romans*, page 241).

That Paul has in mind ecstatic dimensions of the Christian faith in either of these locations is debated. Some scholars wish to reduce to an absolute minimum any positive references in Paul's letters to ecstatic phenomena. But it seems quite likely in both these instances that Paul is incorporating the widespread use of glossolalia in early Christianity into his argument. Whether there is a polemical element in his use of these ideas in 8:26-27 is a problem, however, because Paul does not enter into polemic in Romans in general; and this particular context gives no indication of his rejection of any specific idea. That Paul is in tension with the "enthusiasts" is something that scholars like Ernst Kaesemann assume but have difficulty proving in detail. After all, Paul confesses in 1 Corinthians 14:18, "I thank God that I speak in tongues more than all of you." It is likely, therefore, that he would have considered himself a charismatic and that others in the early church would have perceived him in the same way. Glossolalia as an indication of human weakness, however, is a significant point in Paul's argument. Ecstatic cries are an ultimate expression of human vulnerability as well as a sign that people feel accepted at a deep level that is beyond speech. Therefore it is an integral aspect of Christian experience.

Romans 8:31-39. As we discovered in answering Question 9 in Dimension One, Paul has an elaborate list of the cosmic powers in 8:35-39. In the first century, people believed that the world was dominated by forces and powers in the world around them. They had a personified idea of evil and economics and social forces. They believed that there were powers in the heavens—the "height"—and that there were powers below the surface of the earth—the "depth" (8:39). They were convinced that every human institution was something of the otherworldly power, capable of exercising an evil, superhuman control.

An investigation of this usage by Walter Wink (*Naming the Powers*; Fortress Press, 1984) suggests that the wide variety of terms used for these forces and the fact that so many of them appear to be historical or social powers or factors leads us to a single hypothesis concerning Paul's view. Wink suggests that Paul understood all human institutions as having an inner and an outer side. These institutions and forces have an external structure, but they also have an internal spirit or ethos. We know this to be the case of the institutions for which we work and of the governments that have been established by humans. Each has a different structure; but even those with the same structure have a different kind of spirit, shaped by the persons leading them and shaped by the peculiar history of each institution.

Wink suggests a simple formula for understanding the principalities (experiences) and powers: $P = O + I$. He means that "powers" equals the "outer plus inner" side. With this theory Wink is able to explain how experiences and powers sometimes become evil. They sometimes develop a concept of themselves as absolute. They may begin to call for absolute obedience from those who work in them or serve them. When the institutions of this world are actually revered as superhuman and ultimate, they can become demonic.

Paul's contention in 8:31-39 is that none of these institutions and forces is capable of separating humans from the love of Christ. Although the world remains fallen and these forces remain a reality, Christians have no need to lose heart. They have a basis for final confidence, a relational foundation for hope in the love of God that is demonstrated to us in that God "did not spare his own Son, but gave him up for us all" (8:32). The thrilling sequence at the end of Romans 8 affirms not only the triumphant power of God over all human institutions but also the basis of Christian realism and hope. These forces that are often distorted and cause uncounted evil, contributing to the groaning of the whole creation, do not have ultimate power. They are in the process of transformation. And as Christians become agents of righteousness, their task is to work for the transformation of these forces and institutions. The final transformation, of course, will not occur until the end of time. But in the meanwhile, Paul recommends an attitude that is the opposite of servility toward the principalities and powers of this world. Christians are not to be frightened of them, for they are incapable of separating believers from the love of God.

DIMENSION THREE: WHAT DOES THE BIBLE MEAN TO ME?

The Flesh/Spirit Dualism—The Modern Superhero

Among the areas of the modern world that have been influenced by a sometimes distorted grasp of the flesh/spirit in Romans 8 is the modern superhero. In the classic cowboy stories, the allegiance of the superhero to the higher realm was shown by the superhero resisting such temptations of "the flesh" as gambling, drinking alcohol, and sexual attraction. In more recent forms of the superheroic tales, such resistance is limited to remaining true to the righteous cause. This may also be described as the battle between good and evil, whether on the earthly plane or the cosmic one. The superhero or superheroine will not sell out when the crisis comes and is an embodiment of "the good" (like Superman or Batman, battling for justice) or the Jedi in Star Wars, empowered by "the Force" and battling for the cosmic good by rooting out and destroying the evil. The supervillains, on the other hand, are usually characterized as motivated by pride, arrogance, lust for power, greed, and other fleshly considerations.

The threat of evil in the modern superheroic fantasy is perceived to be caused by villains who are not really part of the democratic community. Thus redemption can occur when such villains are destroyed, restoring the community to a trouble-free situation. In contrast, Romans 8 suggests that the creation continues to groan under the weight of universal human sin even after the coming of Christ to redeem. In contrast to superheroic drama, Paul remains realistic about both the responsibility for and the duration of adversity. The key to redemption for him is the love of Christ that gives us courage in face of the distorted powers of the world, whereas superheroic stories offer a simplistic and illusory escape from threats.

If their rejection brought reconciliation to the world, what will their acceptance be but life from the dead? (11:15).

11

UNBELIEF AND WORLD CONVERSION

Romans 9–11

DIMENSION ONE: WHAT DOES THE BIBLE SAY?

Answer these questions by reading Romans 9–11

1. How many things does Paul list that belong to the people of Israel? What are they? (9:4-5)

   Paul lists eight privileges that belong to Israel. They are the "sonship," "the divine glory," "the covenants," "the receiving of the law," "the temple worship," "the promises," "the patriarchs," and "the Messiah."

2. From whom did the people of Israel descend, from Isaac or from Esau? (9:6-13)

   In 9:7, 10 Paul argues that Israel descended from Isaac and Jacob, not Ishmael or Esau.

3. What does Paul give as the reason why God elects to have mercy on whom God wills? (9:16)

   The reason is to show that God's mercy "does not . . . depend on human desire or effort."

4. Why did Israel not succeed in fulfilling the law? (9:30-32)

   According to 9:32, Israel did not succeed in fulfilling the law "because they pursued it not by faith but as if it were by works."

5. What is the word that is "near you . . . in your mouth and in your heart"? (10:8)

   Paul defines this word as "the message concerning faith that we proclaim."

6. How does Paul say that faith comes? (10:17)

Paul writes that "faith comes from hearing the message, and the message is heard through the word about Christ."

7. Why is Paul convinced that God "did not reject" Israel? (11:1-6)

God has not rejected his people because "at the present time there is a remnant chosen by grace" (not by works).

8. Whom does Paul liken to the "wild olive shoot" grafted into the olive tree? (11:17-24)

When Paul speaks of "you, though a wild olive shoot" (11:17) and contrasts this with "they were broken off" (11:20), identifying the latter as "the natural branches" of the tree (11:21), it is clear that the Gentiles are the wild olive shoot. (See also verse 13.)

9. What is the "mystery" that Paul reveals? (11:25-26a)

The mystery that Paul reveals is that Israel will be hardened "in part until the full number of the Gentiles has come in, and in this way all Israel will be saved."

10. Who does Paul say has actually ever "known the mind of the Lord"? (11:33-36)

Paul implies that only God really knows "the mind of the Lord."

DIMENSION TWO:
WHAT DOES THE BIBLE MEAN?

In Romans 9–11 we turn to material that has often been viewed as only loosely connected with the rest of Paul's letter to the Romans. Particularly to scholars oriented to the Reformation tradition, believing that the purpose of Romans was to teach the proper doctrine of justification by grace alone, the material in these chapters seems quite problematic. Among traditional interpreters, only the Calvinists have taken great pleasure in the content of these chapters and have tried to make a case that they connected closely with Romans. In the approach we are following in this course, an integral relationship between these chapters and the rest of the argument of Romans is presupposed. The proofs that confirm the basic thesis of Romans 1:16-17 are being continued in 9–11. These three chapters are an extended discussion of the plight of Israel as it throws light on the central thesis concerning the righteousness of God.

The three chapters are divided into ten well-organized units. The first is the introduction (9:1-5), describing the tragic riddle of Israel's unbelief. Paul then opens the formal argument with 9:6-18, discussing the fate of Israel and the righteousness of divine election. In this section Israel's destiny is seen to come through Isaac so that the true Israelites are "children of the promise" (9:8). The next section of the argument is 9:19-29, which answers an objection to Paul's argument. If Israel's destiny was the result of divine election, then how can God hold anybody else accountable for failing to perform? Paul deals with this by a series of scriptural proofs concerning the potter and the clay and Israel's uneven relationship with God in the past.

In 9:30–10:4, Paul answers the question about the righteousness of God by a doctrine of unenlightened zeal. Here he shows that Jewish zealotry had resulted in their rejecting the righteousness of God as it came to them in the Christ event. In the fifth section of the argument, 10:5-13, Paul argues that righteousness by faith alone is confirmed by Scripture. In this section he stresses the impartial quality of the righteousness of God, including Jews as well as Gentiles.

In 10:14-21, Paul describes the gospel that was freely preached to the whole world but rejected by some of Israel. Then in 11:1-10, Paul provides an answer as to whether indeed God has rejected Israel. Paul contends that a remnant of Jews has indeed been responsive to the grace of God and that God has in no sense repudiated Israel. In 11:11-24, Paul takes up the issue of the hidden purpose of Israel's rejection of the gospel. The gospel has thereby been proclaimed to Gentiles so that the promise given to Israel (that Israel would be a blessing to the Gentile world) has indeed been fulfilled. The word of God has not been empty.

In the ninth section of the argument, 11:25-32, Paul lays out the "mystery" of Israel's salvation. After the appropriate number of Gentiles has been brought into the church, Paul believes that "all Israel will be saved." The conclusion of the argument, 11:33-36, is a doxology concerning the mysterious mind of God. This ends with a suitable reference to the all-inclusive power and scope of the divine rule and glory (11:36).

Romans 9:1-5. The opening lines of Romans 9 convey the deep sense of personal anguish that Paul had experienced when his fellow Jews repudiated the gospel of Christ. The sincerity of his convictions on this point have apparently been called into question because he refers to his conscience bearing witness to the truth of this anguish. Paul feels so strongly about this that he wishes that he himself were cursed for the sake of his brothers if they could only be included in the Christian fellowship (9:3).

Furthermore, that Paul cannot abandon a Jewish role in the Christian faith is elaborated by his listing the eight privileges that belong to Israel. (See the answer to Question 1 in Dimension One.) Here Paul picks up the rest of the theme that was left over from Romans 3:1-2. He had said at that point in answer to the question of what advantage does the Jew have, "Much in every way!" But in Romans 3, Paul only dealt with one of these advantages, the fact that Israel had been entrusted with the oracles of God. Here Paul lays out all the great contributions of Israel, contributions that were absolutely essential for a proper understanding of the gospel itself.

From this rather elaborate listing of Jewish contributions, we see that Paul does not wish to support an anti-Semitic view of the faith, an issue that was apparently raging in Rome at this time. The Jewish Christians were being discriminated against by the Gentile Christians; and Paul is making a case here that by rejecting Jews, Gentiles are rejecting their own religious heritage. Every one of the eight attributes of the Jewish tradition has played a role in the earlier argument of Romans. Paul cannot conceive of a Christianity apart from Judaism.

The great religious heritage shared by the Jewish people would all be null and void if the faithfulness of God were jeopardized. Paul undertakes to discuss this issue in Romans 9–11. Does the repudiation of the gospel by a part of the Jewish people prove that God's word is not indeed powerful? We have traced this theme throughout Paul's letter, showing its relevance from the moment of its initial statement in the thesis of 1:16-17 that the gospel "is the power of God that brings salvation to everyone." If the gospel is not powerful enough even to convince God's own people, what hope is there for the salvation of the world? And if God cannot prevail and make this word stand, how can salvation be trusted? Thus Romans 9:6 states the fundamental issue to be dealt with in these three chapters, whether "God's word had failed."

After flatly denying that God's word failed, Paul supports his case on the premise that God's promise to Israel, given to Abraham, was that "through Isaac . . . your offspring will be reckoned" (9:7). This citation of an important principle of Jewish theology (Genesis 21:12) is interpreted in such a way that the true children of Isaac are understood to be "children of the promise," persons who have responded to God's word.

Romans 9:6-18. The problem that Paul faces in Romans 9–11 is a formidable one. Is it possible to believe that Israel was elected by God and yet that Israel has stumbled and is now being rejected? If the election of Israel had the power of God behind it, how could it be thwarted by human resistance? Paul deals with this issue in a forthright manner, interpreting the Isaac story in such a way that the election of God continues, "not by works but by him who calls" (9:12). Paul is building a case here that those who rest their reliance on their "works" are not truly the children of Isaac. Only those who see their lives resting entirely on the mercy and the call of God are the true children of Israel. Paul at this point is elaborating the theme that we studied in 2:28-29, that the true Jew is the one who is circumcised in the heart. Similarly, Paul argued in 4:12 that Abraham was the father of those who "follow in the footsteps of the faith that our father Abraham had before he was circumcised."

With this distinction, Paul is able to take seriously the problem of stumbling. That humans had repeatedly rejected the call of God and that Israel in particular had been unfaithful is proved by the Scripture quotations in 9:25-33. In the last of these citations (9:33), Paul correlates stumbling and the avoidance of stumbling with the possession of faith. Therefore God's promise to be faithful to Israel has not been broken. Those who have faith and act as children of the promise remain under the power of God. To them God has remained faithful (9:33).

Paul then goes on to explain this stumbling through a theory of unenlightened zeal that is closely related to his own conversion (10:1-4). We dealt with this theme in Romans 7. Here in 10:3, Paul explicitly correlates the theme of righteousness with the rejection of Christ on the part of zealous Jews. In rejecting Christ, they are seeking to "establish their own [righteousness, and] they did not submit to God's righteousness."

Romans 10:4. The underlying issue in the rejection by zealous Jews of the revelation of the righteousness of God in Christ was the law. The fact that Jesus was a lawbreaker and that he was executed in a way that revealed to popular perception that he was a lawless sinner made the center of the gospel an issue of disrepute among loyal Jews. The statement about the relation between Christ and the law in 10:4, however, is rather complicated and requires some sorting out.

I want to present three possibilities for the translation of the term that is rendered "culmination" or "end" in the New International Versions. That Paul meant to say Christ was "the end of the law" has been most often supported by Lutheran scholars. This approach tends to make law and gospel into absolutely opposing realms. A representative of this view is Ernst Kaesemann, who writes, "The Mosaic Torah comes to an end with Christ" (*Commentary on Romans*, page 283). Others try to correlate this particular translation with the central theme of Pauline theology concerning freedom from the law and justification by grace alone. One tendency of those using this translation is to view Christianity as unalterably opposed to Judaism, to interpret Paul as opposed on principle to the law. Whether intended or not, it is clear that to call the Torah fundamentally into question is to undercut any basis of dialogue with Judaism.

The second view, one favored by Calvinist interpreters and many others, is that the word in 10:4 should be translated as "goal" or "fulfillment." The basic conviction in this translation is that Paul does not really believe Christ has abolished the law and that such statements as "apart from the law" in 3:21 have been grossly exaggerated. The Calvinist preference is to keep the realm of law intact so that there will be a viable basis for reconstructing the human community. Despite this element of theological bias, there appears to be little doubt that this translation fits the context better.

The third approach to the translation of Romans 10:4 is the least acceptable, though it is strongly advocated in some commentaries. The suggestion is that Paul intended the Greek word to mean *both* the end and the goal of the law. One scholar even goes so far as to suggest that Paul was "deliberately using the ambiguity in the word to cover up a subtle change in the direction of his thought on the matter. . . . Paul seems to be implying that, though the function of the law has been radically altered by the coming of Christ, it has not been altogether abolished." I see some major problems with this third alternative. First, Paul's wording of 10:4 gives no hint that he wished to insert an element of ambiguity. Second, I find a serious flaw in terms of method in this third interpretation, which can confuse the alternatives developed in the debate between current scholars with the original intention of Paul.

Several studies of 10:4 have lent weight to the second alternative described above, namely that Paul intended to say that Christ is the *goal* of the law. A thorough investigation of the Greek word behind this translation suggests that originally it meant "apex, aim, or completion." The idea of goal or fulfillment is characteristic of Paul's use of this group of terms.

The consequence of this research is that 10:4 provides a much less polemical basis than usual for the relation between Jews and Christians. Paul's argument in 9:30–10:4 is that the ultimate purpose of the law was that all persons, Jews and Gentiles alike, might find righteousness. If Christ is the "goal of the law," the path of faith can be pursued without repudiating the Torah.

A crucial point here is that no one needs to become anti-Semitic to be a Christian. And Jews need not repudiate their legacy of the Torah if they become Christians. That Paul believes this is clearly indicated by his statement of the eight advantages the Jews have in 9:4-5. It is also strongly confirmed by the formulation Paul used to conclude 3:31: "Rather, we uphold the law." This verse has always given some scholars a terrible time because it seems so flatly to contradict what Paul writes in 10:4. But when 10:4 is understood to say that Christ is the goal of the law, the contradiction disappears.

Romans 10:5-9. The references in Romans 10:5-9 to bringing Christ "up" or "down" may be puzzling to the members of your group. Several citations from the Old Testament are woven together here into an argument that bears directly on the question of gaining righteousness by law, the question that was crucial in Paul's understanding of the misguided zeal of 10:4. Paul acknowledges that the Jews have zeal for the law but that it is "not based on knowledge" (10:2). In trying to establish righteousness by conforming to "works," the zealots have not responded in the right way to the revelation of God's righteousness in the Christ event.

In 10:5-9, Paul argues that the person who is devoted to obeying the law is convicted of the error of that strategy by the law itself. Legalistic obedience that is motivated by the effort to bring the messianic era is defined here as wrong. Romans 10:5 states the basic principle that every person who lives by the law must obey it at every point. And then Deuteronomy 30:12 is cited— "Do not say in your heart, 'Who will ascend into heaven?' (that is, to bring Christ down)"— in order to show that the attempt to bring the Messiah through observing the law is explicitly forbidden by the law. The zealous Jews had assumed that if all Israel would obey the law just for one day, the Messiah would come and vindicate the righteous.

Paul shows that this kind of strategy of bringing in the Messiah is actually sinful now that the Messiah has already come. No longer does anyone need to "ascend into heaven" or "descend into the deep" to inaugurate and defend the messianic age. It has already come in Christ. What is required now, rather than frantic efforts to bring the Kingdom, is an appropriate response to the good news that the Kingdom has already come in Christ.

Paul's Attitude Toward Judaism

The issue of Romans 9–11 and particularly the question of Paul's expectation of the conversion of Jews to Christianity has been widely debated in scholarly circles. In order to provide some orientation for the members of your group, several of the major contributions to this important discussion need to be sketched.

J. Christian Beker deals with the issue of Jews and Gentiles within the context of his contention that Paul's theology was dominated by end-time thinking (*Paul the Apostle: The Triumph of God in Life and Thought*, Fortress Press, 1984). He defends Paul as the only New Testament writer who is passionately engaged with Jews as the people of promise. Although he recognizes that Paul had a different understanding of messianism than the Jewish community as a whole, he insists that Paul was the New Testament writer who most consistently kept "his thought anchored in the Hebrew scriptures and in the destiny of Israel as God's people."

Beker suggests that Paul remained convinced of the priority of Israel, reflected in the repeated line in Romans, "first for the Jew, then for the Gentile" (1:16; 2:9, 10). Beker understands these statements within the context of the Roman community and the argument of the faithfulness of God to Israel. If the promises of God to Israel are annulled, then the inclusion of the Gentiles loses its foundation.

In relation to Romans 9–11, Beker insists that Israel is not expected to be absorbed by the church. When Paul refers to the "mystery" of Israel's salvation (11:25), he is talking about the mysterious dynamic of God's salvation history in which successive periods of Jewish and Gentile disobedience and conversion will finally result in the conversion and unification of the world.

Beker rejects the idea of Jewish conversion to Christianity and calls for a dialogue about the problems of understanding messianism in the modern world. He points out the distinctive feature of Christian messianism as an important issue to be discussed with Jews. From the Christian perspective, "the Messiah has come, but without his kingdom." That is, the fulfillment of the messianic promises is left to the future.

In both his books on Paul, E. P. Sanders has provided a bulwark against an anti-Semitic interpretation; but he does not approve of the rejection of a Jewish mission that marks the work of Beker. (See *Paul and Palestinian Judaism: A Comparison of Patterns of Religion*; Fortress Press, 1977; and *Paul, the Law, and the Jewish People*; Fortress Press, 1983.) Sanders's basic contention is that Paul's critique of Judaism rests entirely on his Christian experience and thus has nothing to do with the actual shape of Jewish practice in the first century. Paul's only criticism of Judaism was that it did not accept Christ. Insisting on the same "entrance requirement" of faith in Christ, both for Jews and for Gentiles, Paul in effect established a kind of third race, the true Israel mentioned in Romans 2 and 4. Sanders, therefore, favors a straightforward reading of Romans 11:25-26, that, according to Paul, the only way to enter the ranks of the saved is by faith in Christ. Sanders goes on to argue that Paul denied two pillars common to all forms of Judaism, the election of Israel and faithfulness to the Mosaic law. I believe this is somewhat difficult to maintain because Paul explicitly affirms the election of Israel in Romans 3:1-2; 9:4-5, 11. Furthermore, Paul defends the legitimacy of the Torah as we have seen in 3:31 and 10:4.

In reviewing this research, I think it is important to keep in mind that in Romans, Paul defends the integrity of Jewish culture and of Jewish Christians. We have seen throughout Romans the interest in defending the "weak" against the "strong." And even though these are not flat identifications of Jewish Christians versus Gentile Christians, Paul's argument results in defending the minority in Rome, which in this instance contained the Jewish Christians. In Romans 14:1–15:13, Paul repudiates the idea of a monochromatic church in which cultural distinctions and theological tendencies need to be obliterated. While I think that Paul hoped for the conversion of Jews to Christianity in the sense of belief in Christ, he did not really insist on their abandonment of the law. In fact, he makes as strong a case as possible in Romans in defense of the law. But he wishes the law to be interpreted in light of Christ.

DIMENSION THREE:
WHAT DOES THE BIBLE MEAN TO ME?

Unenlightened Zeal and the Conversion of the Jews

Probably the two most complicated issues to be discussed in relation to Romans 9–11 are "unenlightened zeal" and the question of the conversion of the Jews. While zealotism was a factor in Jewish rejection of Christianity according to 10:2-3, it has subsequently played a major role in

Christian persecutions of the Jews. In the ferocity of the Nazi Holocaust, a secular form of this same zealotism resulted in the deaths of millions of Jews, placing a permanent burden on the relations between Christians and Jews. Since the Holocaust, with the rise of Islamic and Christian fundamentalism, unenlightened zeal is resulting in new forms of anti-Semitism. In this situation there is a need for sensitivity in interpreting Romans 9–11. It is time that Christians recognized that their traditional attempts to fulfill Paul's expectation in Romans 11:25-26 by trying to convert Jews has often aimed, in fact, at cultural annihilation. Nothing in Romans provides warrant for the assumption that Jews will accept a Gentile gospel, abandoning their culture of the Torah. Such an assumption is itself a form of "unenlightened zeal," an effort to "establish the righteousness" of later Christian culture by absorbing others.

The issue of the salvation of the Jews thus calls Christians to rethink our entire approach to evangelism. In our Bible studies and mission boards, we need to create modern embodiments of Paul's hope of a generous and inclusive gospel that will counter zealous fanaticism, honor cultural and theological differences, and unite the fractured world. Just as in the case of the Roman house churches, the ones who need to stand first in line for such conversion are we Christians ourselves.

As you sort through these ideas, start the conversation by asking, what form might an enlightened evangelism take in today's pluralistic world?

Love must be sincere. Hate what is evil; cling to what is good (12:9).

12

THE LOVE ETHIC AS RESPONSE

Romans 12

DIMENSION ONE: WHAT DOES THE BIBLE SAY?

Answer these questions by reading Romans 12

1. In view of what does Paul appeal to the Romans? (12:1)
  Paul appeals to the Romans "in view of God's mercy."

2. What does Paul urge the Romans to offer to God? (12:1)
  Paul urges the Romans to present their "bodies as a living sacrifice, holy and pleasing to God."

3. How should the Roman Christians act toward the world? (12:2)
  Paul tells the Roman Christians not to conform to the world, but to be transformed by the renewal of their minds.

4. What points does Paul draw from the metaphor of the body? (12:4-8)
  "In Christ we, though many, form one body" (12:5), and different gifts should be used by members "according to the grace given to each of us" (12:6-8).

5. How many commands does Paul relate in developing the theme "Love must be sincere"? (12:9-20)
  When we count the imperative verbs in this passage, we find two in verse 9 (hate, cling), followed by ten commands in 12:10-13 that spell out aspects of Christian love (be devoted to one another, honor one another, never be lacking in zeal, keep your spiritual fervor, serve the Lord, rejoice in hope, be patient, be faithful, share, practice hospitality). The twelve commands

in 12:14-20 deal more generally with relations to outsiders or members of other Christian house churches (bless, do not curse, rejoice, mourn, live in harmony, do not be proud, do not be conceited, do not repay evil for evil, do what is right, live at peace, never avenge, leave room for God's wrath). [Note that the command about avenging is supported by a citation from Proverbs 25:21-22 so that the commands in that citation (12:20) are not counted as coming directly from Paul.] Finally, 12:21 has a double exhortation (do not be overcome by evil; overcome evil with good). The grand total is therefore twenty-six. [Going through these commands will aid in comprehending the thought and structure of this passage.]

6. Check the Old Testament citation in Romans 12:19. Is the wording "It is mine to avenge; I will repay" closer to Leviticus 19:18 or to Deuteronomy 32:35?

    Romans 12:19 is cited more directly from Deuteronomy 32:35.

7. Romans 12:20 is an exact citation from Proverbs 25:21-22, except that one phrase is left out. What important theme in Romans would have been weakened if this phrase had been cited by Paul?

    The final clause in Proverbs 25:22, "and the LORD will reward you," is deleted by Paul. The central theme of Romans, salvation by grace alone, would be weakened by the inclusion of this clause promising a reward for good works.

8. Verse 21 is considered a summary of the preceding passage. In which verses of Romans 12 do you find the themes of good/evil and overcoming the world rather than being overcome by it?

    "Good/evil" are found in verses 2, 9, and 17. The theme of allowing the world to dominate your thought and behavior is stated in verse 2. It is implied in verses 14; 17; and, as Dimension Two will explain, also in 12:3.

DIMENSION TWO: WHAT DOES THE BIBLE MEAN?

Structure

When you teach Romans 12, you may need to counter the tendency to see this material as unrelated to the earlier argument of Romans and also as a rather disorganized list of exhortations. The material is tightly organized and divided into three sections. (1) Romans 12:1-2 has a thematic statement that sets the tone for the whole ethical section of Romans that extends to 15:7.

(2) Next we find a series of admonitions related to the proper exercise of Christian gifts within the church, Romans 12:3-8. (3) Finally, in 12:9-21, Paul gives us admonitions to express authentic love in the struggle between good and evil. Verses 9 and 21 serve as brackets for this passage, with the admonitions in verses 10-13 dealing primarily with life within a particular congregation and verses 14-20 dealing primarily with relations to persons outside one's particular Christian group. This section is concluded with verse 21, which not only refers to verse 9 but also sums up the themes of the entire chapter.

Romans 12:1-2. Romans 12:1-2 provides the earliest systematic basis for a Christian ethic. The important thing to explain is that the motivation for good behavior developed in these two verses comes from the entire first eleven chapters of Romans, as summarized by the expression "God's mercy." The tendency in the history of interpreting Romans has been to separate the theological section (Romans 1–11) from the ethical section (Romans 12–15). This way of viewing Romans reduces everyday behavior to a position of secondary importance and defines Christianity primarily as a set of beliefs. This view also misinterprets Paul's intent, as seen by the fact that he makes important ethical references in the so-called "dogmatic chapters" of Romans (see 2:21-23; 6:12-19; 7:5-23; 8:3-13) and gives many theological details in the ethical chapters.

Given this tendency to separate ethics from its source, we need to interpret each admonition in the next chapters in light of the summary of 12:1-2. This summary requires us to think of the implications of justification by grace and the function of human gratitude, which contrast so strikingly with conformity to this world. Paul's appeal "in view of God's mercy" assumes that the Romans have experienced the reconciling love of God and are thereby capable of passing that love on to others.

Romans 12:3-8. The contrast in Romans 12:3 between "soberminded" and "superminded" (see the new translation of this verse in the participant book), conveyed in the elaborate play on the word *mind* (used four times in this sentence), would have been easily understood by educated people in the congregation. Greek philosophers had developed a negative evaluation of the superminded heroes like Achilles and Ajax, whose exploits and pride violated standards of decency. The Greeks had a positive attitude toward the soberminded heroes like Odysseus, who resisted pride and accepted limits. The well-known Delphic oracle is related to this contrast: "Know thyself . . . that thou art but mortal," which means knowing you are not a superhero and thus should follow sobermindedness.

Paul was tapping this Greek tradition (similar at some points to the Judaic heritage of pride going before the fall) because his experience had apparently shown him that persons who believe they are gods are impossible to live with. The tendency he is countering in Romans 12:3 is for early Christians to infer from their charismatic experiences that they are divine and thus that others should submit to their domination.

Paul develops in 12:3 the unique idea of an individual's "measuring rod of faith" (again, see the participant book translation), understood as a kind of measuring device by which ethical and theological judgments can be reached. Each Christian is given a unique experience of faith as the Spirit makes the gospel of divine love relevant to the condition of the heart. This measuring rod of faith must be kept by each Christian as the basis of a proper relationship with God and the world.

But if one becomes "superminded" about one's measuring rod, the typical result is to coerce others to accept one's theology and ethical judgments.

A comparison between the body metaphor in 12:4-5 and 1 Corinthians 12:12-27 might help. Since First Corinthians was written several years before Romans, most commentators interpret the latter in light of the former. Actually, some important differences should be taken into account. Not only is the treatment much longer in First Corinthians, its focus is quite different. What begins as a metaphor in 1 Corinthians 12:12 ends up as a realistic identification of the church as the body of Christ in 12:27. This identification is avoided in Romans, where Paul states that the church members who are many form one body in Christ. For some reason Paul does not use the idea of the church as the mystical body of Christ in Romans. Rather than stressing that individuals are part of Christ, he says in Romans 12:5 that "each member belongs to all the others." The most likely explanation of this shift in Romans is that Paul was guarding against "superminded" pretensions that certain gifted believers shared Christ's divinity and thus deserved the status of being the "body of Christ." The stress in Romans is clearly on the equality and interdependence of members with other members.

Romans 12:9-21. In dealing with Romans 12:9-21, decide whether to follow several commentators in viewing the individual admonitions as a random collection of traditional sayings. The reference material here and in the participant book relates the admonitions to the prologue of 12:1-2 and to the brackets of 12:9 and 21, but you may find this unconvincing. The assumption behind the treatment in the participant book is that Paul has selected, adapted, and carefully organized early Christian admonitions to fit the circumstances in the Roman congregation. If you accept this approach, lead a discussion of the relation of the sayings to that congregational situation; if not, then discuss the general significance of the individual sayings for early Christianity.

Some members of your group may be interested in an additional clarification of the different types of love in this passage. The participant book identifies the reference in 12:9 as *agape*, the usual early Christian term for generous, self-giving love that demands nothing in return. The following verse uses the term *philadelphia* and should be translated literally, "having affection for one another with brotherly love." This term implies familial love that is reciprocal. Brothers and sisters share a love derived from common experiences, prolonged intimacy in one family, and common interests in the family's success and reputation. Unfortunately, both terms are translated with a single English word, *love*. Paul uses *agape* for the general admonition in 12:9, whose implications are spelled out in the next several chapters.

Paul resists the tendency to view generous, self-giving love as incompatible with ethical discrimination; if love is unearned and undiscriminating, how can it say no to anything? Paul rejects this approach by demanding that love be "sincere," as proved by its capacity to hate evil and to hold fast to the good. The emotional intensity of these verbs would be more properly conveyed by the literal translation "abhor" and "cleave" rather than "hate" and "cling." Paul obviously holds that the genuineness of *agape* can be measured by the intensity of the repulsion against whatever harms loved ones and of attachment to what preserves their lives. In 12:10, *philadelphia* is a more homey form of love that Paul feels would be suitable for the house churches in Rome, which in fact were treating one another as enemies rather than as brothers and sisters.

Romans 12:16 fits in smoothly with the need for harmony among Christian groups in Rome, but its translation is somewhat confusing and may raise questions in the mind of your group members. The commands "do not be proud" and "do not be conceited" seem to overlap. The same verbal element used four times in the word play of 12:3 appears here. It is visible as the term *mind* in the following literal translation of 12:16:

> Be of the same mind toward one another. Do not set your minds on exalted things but be drawn to lowly persons. Never be wise minded in yourselves.

This admonition is directed to the "superminded" (12:3) members of the congregation. Their attention is so fixed on "exalted" mysteries that they act in condescending ways toward unsophisticated members of the congregation. By requesting that they be "of the same mind toward one another," Paul aims to replace this dangerous sense of superiority with an admission of equality. The church cannot reflect "sincere love" (12:9) if it allows the intellectual and social distinctions of the fallen world to define the status of its members. This verse is important for Sunday school classes where gradations of intelligence and education are often barriers to real communication among equals.

To understand the background of Paul's discussion of vengeance in 12:19-20, we must realize that large segments of the Jewish community in the period prior to the Jewish-Roman war of AD 66–73 favored a vigilante strategy. Modeling their behavior on the heroic tales in the Old Testament, they believed that their vengeance against evildoers would achieve divine ends. In particular, these advocates of Jewish vigilantism felt that the Roman governing authorities should be opposed on principle and with force. And it was natural in this kind of environment that many persons who had suffered injustices at the hands of the authorities felt called by the heroic myth to take the law into their own hands, to avenge themselves, and thus to avenge Israel.

In this context Paul's admonition "Do not take revenge, my dear friends, but leave room for God's wrath" (12:19) assumes significance. He is tapping the ancient tradition of never being a judge in one's own cause, a principle embodied in Jewish as well as in Greco-Roman law. This principle is crucial for modern jurisprudence as well. The trouble with the police or private citizens taking the law into their own hands is that the omniscience and impartiality of the heroic stories never seem to work out in reality. Zealotism is presumptuous, Paul implies here, for it refuses to give way to the prerogatives of divine justice. "Leave room for God's wrath, for it is written: 'It is mine to avenge; I will repay,' says the Lord."

The most significant question we have to face in regard to vengeance is what to do in the meanwhile. If we simply harbor our hatred and fail to express it, we sicken; or if we give way to our desire for vengeance and take the law into our own hands, we suffer disastrous consequences. So Paul's alternative is worth taking seriously.

In place of zealous vigilantism, Paul advises two things: an active concern for the life and well-being of one's adversary and submission to lawful governmental authority (Romans 13:1-7). At first glance these appear to be flatly contradictory, an issue we will take up in Lesson 13.

The concern for the good of one's enemies is dealt with first: Romans 12:20 specifies what was meant earlier in this chapter by the admonition "Do not repay anyone evil for evil" (12:17). Whereas the natural tendency is to respond to violence with violence, to meanness with reprisals, the actions of mercy aim to break the deadly cycle. The abiding guideline of the church is the commitment to "overcome evil with good," as the following verses (12:18-21) set forth.

The strategy Paul recommends seeks not only the well-being but also the transformation of persecutors and criminals. "Do not be overcome by evil, but overcome evil with good" (12:21). This is not to say that what one aims to achieve will actually be accomplished in every instance. Those commentators who accuse Paul of being an incurable optimist in these verses confuse, in my opinion, intentions with results. As Paul knew from personal experience, some adversaries react to being shamed by such unanticipated gestures of love by redoubling the intensity of their hatred. In the final analysis, what one aims to achieve is what is important: transformation, not vengeance.

DIMENSION THREE: WHAT DOES THE BIBLE MEAN TO ME?

Why Should I Do the Good?

The most important question in ethics is, "Why should I do the good?" Paul is much more careful to construct a consistent answer than most modern teachers or preachers. They tend to fall back into the language of conformity and earning acceptance through good works. One way to conduct a discussion of this matter would be to invite participants to share their reactions to moral appeals in the past and to compare them with the appeal in Romans. The contrast between the law and the gospel that we studied earlier in the course might be useful at this point. The most common ethical appeals today are based on new forms of the law. The point that needs to be made is that a healthier appeal would be based on the gospel of "God's mercy."

Vengeance

Romans 12 at several points touches on one of the most troubling aspects of current American culture, the superheroic type of entertainment that makes vengeance popular. These stories began in the 1930s from a long tradition of fascination with vigilantism that has some similarities to the Jewish zealotism of Paul's time. We have long had an ideal of holy vengeance. Acting on the premise that God inspires and justifies the righteous to take vengeance in his behalf, we have celebrated many heroes who took the law into their own hands.

The vigilante ethos justifies direct violence so long as the evil is clear-cut, the vigilantes are disinterested, and their identity is kept secret. The appeal of this vigilante tradition has been that we could gain quick, public vengeance for terrible crimes that might otherwise go unpunished.

An example of this kind of story is *The Virginian*—Owen Wister's novel of 1902 that has the first main street duel in American literature. (This material about *The Virginian* is adapted from Robert Jewett and John Shelton Lawrence, *The American Monomyth*; Doubleday, 1977; pages 180-85.) The story is set in the context of the struggles in Wyoming between farmers and ranchers, specifically the range war in Johnson County, in which lynching and systematic thievery practiced by both sides came to a climax in 1892. The ranchers imported a trainload of Texas gunmen equipped with dynamite to put down the farmers who were homesteading land in the public domain that the ranchers had used without rent for years. The conflict came to a climax when federal troops finally intervened.

Wister took the ranchers' side of this struggle and created the Virginian, a tall, nameless cowboy who became the foreman of Sunk Creek Ranch. He was forced to track down a rustling gang, capturing two of its members, one of whom was formerly his best friend. True to the vigilante code, the Virginian renounced friendship and hanged the thieves. The chief rustler, Trampas, escaped with a guileless sidekick. When the trackers approached, Trampas shot his sidekick in the back so Trampas could escape on their only horse.

Several years later, Trampas rides past the Virginian and his fiancée, Molly the schoolteacher, who comments that it seems "wicked that this murderer" got off when others were hanged for rustling. "He was never even arrested," says the girl. "No, he helped elect the sheriff in that county," replies the Virginian.

In the dramatic climax of the novel, which once was required reading for high school classes all over America, the rustler issues a formal challenge for a main street duel. The Virginian seeks the counsel of the clergyman who planned to perform his and Molly's wedding. The bishop is convinced that the rustlers have to be dealt with by vigilante tactics, that "they elected their men to office, and controlled juries; that they were a staring menace to Wyoming. His heart was with the Virginian. But there was his Gospel that he preached, and believed, and tried to live." He reminds the Virginian of the biblical injunction not to kill. The heroic cowboy responds, "Mighty plain to me, seh. Make it plain to Trampas, and there'll be no killin'."

As they parry about the contradictory demands of religion and law, the Virginian poses the key question: "How about instruments of providence, seh?" In other words, what about the biblical idea of providence taking the form of heroic vigilantes who rid the world of evildoers? The hero reluctantly departs for the duel that means the end of his hoped-for marriage as well as possibly of his life. The bishop finds he cannot repress the words, "God bless him! God bless him!"

The end of the story is so well known that your group members may know it without having read the novel or seen the film *High Noon* in which Gary Cooper played the title role. In an archetypal duel with Trampas, the bad guy draws and shoots first but is killed by the Virginian's bullet. The hero's friends marvel, "You were that cool! That quick!" which is an expression of the cool ethos of the vigilante tradition. The state of Wyoming is redeemed from the threat of crime because vengeance has occurred. Molly's New England conscience, which had resisted the vigilante tactic so strongly, finally relents; and she marries the Virginian. The novel ends with the hero and his family ensconced in prosperity and long life. The Virginian becomes a wealthy rancher and mine owner, passing the redemptive task on to the next generation.

This novel had hundreds of imitations; and shortly after its cinematic triumph in 1929, it was followed by the emergence of serialized stories featuring the supercowboy "The Lone Ranger," the supercop "Dick Tracy," and the superheroes like "Superman" and "Captain America"—tales that embody the same kind of plot. *The Virginian* is one of the most formative tales in American culture, giving shape to the yearning for quick and effective public vengeance without using constitutional means. Here is vengeance without due process of law, yet done with dignity and heroic self-restraint. It allows us to see ourselves gaining vengeance against our enemies, but not exactly by our own doing. The public does not take the law into its own hands in this kind of story; heroes do it in our behalf. "Instruments of providence" take up the task of the "wrath of God" that Paul believed should never be shouldered by us in our own behalf.

Love does no harm to a neighbor. Therefore love is the fulfillment of the law (13:10).

13

A TOLERANT ETHIC IN A NEW ERA

Romans 13:1–15:7

DIMENSION ONE: WHAT DOES THE BIBLE SAY?

Answer these questions by reading Romans 13:1–15:7

1. Where does Paul say that governmental authority comes from? (13:1)
   Paul says that all governmental authority has been established by God.

2. How does Paul suggest that citizens respond to their fear of governmental authority? (13:3)
   Paul writes that by doing "what is right" you will receive the approval of the authorities.

3. The term *wrath* is used in 13:4-5. Can you recall where in Romans this idea is fully developed?
   "The wrath of God" is the topic of 1:18–2:16, with the term appearing in 1:18; 2:5; and 2:8. Wrath *also is found in these verses: 3:5; 4:15; 5:9; 9:22; and 12:19.*

4. What are the four forms of obligation to the Roman government Paul mentions? (13:7)
   Paul directs his readers to pay taxes, revenue, respect, and honor to the authorities to whom these are due.

5. What single obligation does Paul lift up for Christians that provides fulfillment of the law? (13:8, 10)
   Paul holds up love as the "fulfillment of the law."

6. On the basis of 13:11-12, when does Paul expect the return of Christ? (a) Very soon? (b) In another generation? (c) In the far distant future?

    Paul expects Christ to return very soon; "salvation is nearer now than when we first believed."

7. How many times is the relation of the believer to the Lord mentioned in 14:5-9?

    Paul describes the believer's relation to the Lord nine times—five times in 14:6, three times in 14:8, and once in 14:9.

8. What are the three aspects of the "kingdom of God"? (14:17)

    The kingdom of God is "righteousness, peace and joy in the Holy Spirit."

9. The summary in 15:7 calls for Christians to "accept one another." Where was this point made earlier in this lesson? (14:1, 3)

    This point was made in the introductory exhortation in the discussion of the "weak" and the "strong" (14:1). Also Paul affirms that "God has accepted them" (14:3).

DIMENSION TWO: WHAT DOES THE BIBLE MEAN?

The material in Romans 13:1–15:7 provides guidelines for living in righteousness in relation to the problems the Roman house churches faced. This passage deals with the issue of the government in a way that has always been controversial in the United States. Since this section ends with an exhortation (15:7) that serves beautifully to summarize the theological and ethical argument of the entire letter, this is appropriate material for the end of our study.

The structure of the material is fairly easy to discern. Romans 13:1-7 deals with the issue of proper subjection to the government. Romans 13:8-10 sets forth the relation of love to law. Romans 13:11-14 describes and calls for moral alertness in the final days. Romans 14:1-28 provides guidelines for the weak and the strong and for mutual upbuilding in the congregation. Romans 15:1-6 provides an exhortation to follow Christ's example in accepting outsiders into the church. Finally, 15:7 draws the preceding argument together and opens the conclusion of the formal argument of the letter, which deals with world mission and unification.

In particular, draw group members' attention to the highly relevant rationale that Paul provides for tolerance within the Christian community. Given the fact that the question of mutual welcome between competitive branches of Christianity is such a problem in the modern period, this material has a practical relevance in showing the concrete bearing of Paul's argument on life today.

Romans 13:1-7. From the perspective of those committed to a modern democratic society, the argument in 13:1-7 is a problem. We experienced the impact of this in early American history. At the time of the American Revolution, the Tories, who were preaching against the revolution, argued on the basis of these verses for loyalty to King George III. In contrast, the preachers advocating rebellion took their texts from the Old Testament or other parts of the New Testament. This example could be duplicated many times in Western Christianity. In general, conservatives and defenders of the divine right of kings have appreciated these verses; reformers and democratic theorists have not. Taken out of context and interpreted from a literal perspective, these words have even provided support for vicious dictators. The "German Christians" in the 1930s and 1940s argued that Adolph Hitler was one "instituted" by God who did not "bear the sword for no reason" (13:2-4).

While the historical circumstances at the time of Paul's writings and the context in Romans 13 throw light on the situation, likely the members of your group will continue to be divided in their understanding of how these verses should be taken by the democratic society. The difference between our situation and that faced by Paul is substantial. The members of the Roman house churches, with minor exceptions, had no direct voice in governmental affairs. Even those who were involved in the bureaucracy had nothing like the kind of autonomy that we would expect in the modern world. No Christian voted that government into existence or selected its current emperor. The situation is vastly different in the modern world where, in our situation at least, the government is established by popular will and governmental authorities are routinely elected by popular vote. In a very real sense, we are the government in this society in a way that was inconceivable for the ancient world. This vast difference in circumstance needs to be taken into account as your group discusses Romans 13. Perhaps the wisdom of Ernst Kaesemann, the German scholar who struggled against Fascism and has written a major investigation of Romans 13:1-7, would be useful. Kaesemann writes,

> When a new situation is set up . . . by a democratic system, Paul's true concern, namely, that God be served in the political sphere as well, is not invalidated. But it does not tolerate holding fast to antiquated slogans, nor is it fostered by an outdated metaphysics. The old demand must be grasped in terms of the new reality and its problems, and applied to these. Paul is confident that the charismatic community can do this (*Commentary on Romans*, page 359).

Several studies have thrown light on the historical circumstances that led to Paul's remarkably positive appraisal of government authority at the time of the mid-50s in the first century. Studies by Marcus Borg and Peter Stuhlmacher are particularly relevant. (See details in *Christian Tolerance*, by Robert Jewett; Westminster, 1982; pages 114–20.) Borg shows that the Jewish community in Rome had some "anti-Roman sentiments" that led it to agree with the Zealot resistance movement in Israel. Borg feels that Paul's major thrust in these verses, therefore, was that Christians should not extend their loyalty to Israel so far that it ended up in hostility against Rome. The message of Romans is that Christ has bridged the chasm between the nations. The

Roman authority in this time, therefore, should be viewed as coming from the same God who was the God of the Israelite nation.

Borg goes on to suggest that the phrase "bear the sword" in 13:4 refers to the military and war-making ability of the Roman state rather than to its judicial punishment system. This point is rather a problem, however, because the Roman legions, which were entrusted with the defense of the frontier and military preparedness, also acted as police and judicial agents. Capital punishment in the Greco-Roman world was carried out by the military officers of the Roman legions.

Professor Stuhlmacher and his colleagues discovered a correlation between the wording about taxation in 13:6-7 and agitation in the Nero administration concerning overly high taxes. This agitation was to some degree public and may well have attracted the sympathy of the members of Roman house churches. In light of the troubles the churches had experienced with the edict of Claudius and the difficulty Jewish Christians were having in returning to Rome, Paul was suggesting that it would be unwise to get involved in potentially subversive tax resistance activities.

Another consideration in interpreting Romans 13:1-7 is that, during the period when Paul wrote, the Roman Empire had an exemplary form of law enforcement. The Nero administration was largely controlled by Seneca and Burrus, who were fair and efficient in their conduct of the law. At the time Paul was writing, the conspiracy laws had been abolished and the arbitrary death penalties for potential subversives that had marked the period before and after this time had been abandoned. Compared, in fact, with the lawlessness that Paul had experienced at the hands of zealots from the Jewish tradition, the Roman administration of law in the mid-50s looked as if it would be a positive ally of Christianity. This situation was drastically changed after AD 62 when Nero's administration became paranoid and the conspiracy laws were reenacted. Two years later, the first serious persecution of Christians at the hands of Roman authorities occurred after the fire of Rome. Nero was apparently directly involved in this vicious persecution, which set the precedent for a number of other persecutions for the next three hundred years.

Paul was not a fortune-teller, and he had no way of knowing that the Roman authorities that he placed such confidence in in the winter of 56–57 would turn so vicious a mere six years later. One of the questions that you might discuss with participants is whether they believe Paul might have formulated his argument differently after AD 62.

Romans 14:1-12. The underpinning for Paul's argument in favor of mutual tolerance is the idea of the lordship of Christ. One sees this first in the theme of the "master" of servants in 14:4. It is developed in an elaborate way in verses 5-9, as the members of your group have discovered in answering Question 7 in Dimension One. This theme was basic for early Christianity. The earliest Christian confession was that "Jesus is Lord." The idea of redemption as developed in Romans has as its premise that Christ has set people free from false lords and has now become their graceful Master. This theme is also strongly correlated with "righteousness," which prevails when the lordship of God is manifest. One finds this in early Christian hymns dealing with the bending of every knee to Christ in the Final Judgment. Paul uses precisely this line in his quotation in 14:11.

An important teaching of the lordship of Christ for early Christianity was that believers are truly subject to no one else. Even the power of the Roman government, as we saw in 13:1-7, is derivative. That authority is given by God. Therefore Christians are not to feel subservient to anyone. This teaching has a particular bearing on the competitive situation among the house churches in Rome because each group was acting like the lord of the other. In a very real sense, intolerance threatens the lordship of Christ. Or to place it in the framework of Jewish theology, refusing to recognize that it is "to their own master [that] servants stand or fall" (14:4) is a challenge to the sovereignty of God and thus a violation of the first and second commandments.

A proper grasp of the theme of lordship and its correlation with the first and second commandments allows one to see the basis for Paul's strenuous argument in favor of tolerance in Rome. The first commandment, that one should have no other gods before God, stresses as Paul does here that we should not play the role of lords to one another. To judge or despise one's competitors therefore violates the first commandment, representing the human effort to become God rather than to recognize and worship the one true God. This teaching is particularly difficult to grasp in a religious community where the basis of judging and despising is understood to be loyalty to God.

The second commandment, that one should refrain from worshiping graven images, guards the transcendent God from any idolatrous human definitions. In a sense, the competing house churches in Rome were each struggling for theological and ethical forms of graven images. They were making their definition of the truth final, demanding that others submit to it.

In light of Paul's argument in 14:1-12, we are able to see that tolerant pluralism can only be preserved when the tension between the first and second commandments is respected. Here is a summary of this argument from my book *Christian Tolerance: Paul's Message to the Modern Church*:

> Faith without tolerance violates the Second Commandment, making a graven image out of some finite definition of the transcendent. Tolerance without faith violates the First Commandment, refusing to choose the God who stands transcendent above all lesser realities. Zealous fanaticism thus violates the Second Commandment, while relativism and nihilism violate the First. Healthy tolerance is the social corollary of a faith that retains the discipline of both the First and the Second Commandment (page 69).

In Paul's view, the lordship of Christ, understood in the context of the first two commandments, provided a bulwark against the conflict among Christian groups that was jeopardizing the world mission and unification of the Christian community.

Defining Tolerance

I have used the term *tolerance* repeatedly to describe the thrust of Paul's argument in Romans 14:1–15:7. This modern term that came into use in Western civilization after the Reformation is not actually used in Paul's argument. When Paul speaks of "acceptance," he has a considerably more active and friendly attitude in mind than is usually conveyed by our modern term *tolerance*.

Yet if the practical significance of Paul's argument is to be understood, we must relate it to the discussion of tolerance in our society.

Two broad types of tolerance have emerged over the last several centuries. "Formal tolerance" is based on closing one's eyes to the doctrinal issues or the personal convictions of persons who disagree with us. One finds this attitude in the Enlightenment and in the political arrangements for tolerance that fall under the definition of the separation of church and state. This kind of formal tolerance is advocated by John Locke, John Stuart Mill, and modern liberalism. Formal tolerance assumes that humans cannot know the final truth and that it is better for them to avoid conflicts on issues that cannot be settled. This tradition suggests that issues of conscience should be relegated to the private sphere and that government authorities so far as possible should avoid intervening in this sphere. The expression of erroneous ideas is to be tolerated by the state because it is too risky for the state to try to determine the complex theological and personal issues of life. The best the state can do is to preserve freedom of religion and conscience, allowing persons to do as they please so long as they do not injure others.

The form of tolerance that comes out of this tradition is very much "live and let live." It is expressed in what current-day sociologists call "civility." Our society, in fact, has had some fairly elaborate rules of civility that used to include not discussing delicate and controversial issues, such as religion. In general, this rule still exists in our society, perhaps more among local groups and conversations, and less so publicly, it seems, as polarized groups are more emboldened to advocate loudly for their diverse ideologies, including "religious" bases for their positions (regardless how of good or faulty their theology). When Americans refrain from discussing the intricate theological assumptions of one another's systems, it may be because we are so uninformed on the particulars. We are willing to talk about the superficial aspects of someone else's religion, often heard through the media, regardless of how accurate, but often avoid discussing the basics or engaging in meaningful conversation with people who really do know. We learn the polite smile and the shrug that allow us to hear offensive opinions, either without being particularly bothered or influenced by them or by gritting our teeth and venting in a more agreeable arena. These rituals of civility let us live as a pluralistic society with a measure of surface tranquility.

Paul's concept is much closer to what some people have called "actual positive tolerance" or "intrinsic tolerance." This kind of tolerance is often found in mystical religious traditions both inside and outside the Christian heritage. This tradition recognizes that other persons whose convictions differ from ours have genuine encounters with the sacred. In this type of tolerance, the basis is the mysterious realm of divine truth that no system of dogmas can encompass. Persons who are grounded in this mystical truth are tolerant so long as they are able to distinguish between "truth as experienced reality" and "truth as rational correctness." That is, persons who approach tolerance this way can recognize the truth that other people have experienced; but they recognize that such truths cannot finally be defined in rational terms.

Unlike the mystics who promote "intrinsic tolerance," Paul believes in a publicly accessible revelation of the love of God in the Christ event. He sets forth in Romans the idea that no humans can justify themselves by conforming to their own principles. Therefore their lives must rest on

God's gift to them. Since they are "accepted" unconditionally by God, they are given the power and the admonition to pass such acceptance on to others. Paul's concept of tolerance is "actual" and "positive." Paul's concept is also more strenuous and forthright about its assumptions than the philosophical tradition is often willing to believe. Paul offers in Romans a way of correlating tolerance with faith. Those who have faith in the "rightwising" activity of God in Christ recognize that God has treated them tolerantly. The love that has been poured into them is capable of being expressed to others because the barriers are destroyed and a new basis of community is achieved.

The horizons of Pauline tolerance, of course, are within the Christian community itself. Paul does not envision the kind of social tolerance that we enjoy in the modern world, though in a real sense the Roman Empire at this time was offering a kind of live-and-let-live opportunity. If we wish to extend Paul's theory of tolerance into the social ground today, we can only do so by analogy. But it should be acknowledged that the most difficult areas for tolerance are in fact within believing communities themselves.

Given the wide range of beliefs between "right" and "left" in many religions, and the attendant growing distrust and hostility, religious toleration may be more comfortable among those at similar places on the conservative-liberal scale, rather than within highly polarized religious groups (though superficially, at least, those on the farthest left of any religion seem not to like anyone but themselves). Therefore, Paul's argument for tolerance in Romans has a resource that extends far beyond the bounds of the Christian community itself. If Christian churches could find here a rationale for a new style of internal interaction, they would likely also gain the capacity to treat persons outside their community with new dignity and compassion. In a real sense Paul's hope of unifying the human race under Christ can only be accomplished when the Christian community itself begins to exhibit the kind of mutual acceptance that ultimately is intended for the whole created order.

Glory and Righteousness

At two points in our material for this week's lesson, Paul provides summary statements that draw the themes of his entire letter together. One of these is 14:17: "For the kingdom of God is not a matter of eating and drinking, but of righteousness, peace and joy in the Holy Spirit." We have repeatedly pointed to righteousness and "rightwising" as the central theme of Romans and have noted earlier how the motif of "peace" dominates the argument in Romans 5 and 15. That believers are given peace with God in the form of reconciling love, overcoming their hostility against God and other humans, is the central result of the gospel. This peace has a direct bearing on the Roman house church situation, and it is no accident that Paul identifies God as the "God of peace" in 15:33. Joy in the Holy Spirit is the human response to the gift of righteousness and peace, a response that Paul expects in the mission shortly to encompass the world. "Rejoice, you Gentiles, with his people" (15:10).

Closely associated with this great summary in 14:17 is the one in 15:7, which is developed in the participant book at some length. To live for the glory of God in the context of the struggle in Rome would mean to give up claims to have the total truth and the insistence that everyone else agree. The tolerant welcome among the members of the house churches would reveal that God's glory rather than the glory of individual groups was now manifesting itself. One commentator describes the significance of this theme in the following words: "The work of Christ for Jews and Gentiles alike served the glory of God, in order that both, Jews and Gentiles, would be able to praise God, in the same congregation, with one accord and one voice."

The significance of this unique correlation between mutual tolerance and the glory of God is visible when you recognize how distinct Paul's view was in comparison with the rest of the biblical tradition. Many Jewish and Christian writers assumed that God's glory would only be manifest with the total victory of good over evil. One sees this, for example, in Psalm 79:6-10, where the psalmist asks God to pour out wrath on

> . . . the nations
>   that do not acknowledge you,
> on the kingdoms
>   that do not call on your name;
> for they have devoured Jacob
>   and devastated his homeland.

The psalmist asks for God's direct intervention:

> Help us, God our Savior,
>   for the glory of your name;
> deliver us and forgive our sins. . . .
> Before our eyes, make known among the nations
>   that you avenge the outpoured blood of your servants.

Here the glory of God is manifest when God triumphs over foreign enemies. Those who have held Israel captive will be punished vengefully. And when that vengeance takes place, Israel will be restored and God's name will be glorified. The more active form of this traditional approach to glory is found in Psalm 149:5-9:

> Let the faithful people rejoice in this honor
>   and sing for joy on their beds.
> May the praise of God be in their mouths
>   and a double-edged sword in their hands,
> to inflict vengeance on the nations
>   and punishment on the peoples,
> to bind their kings with fetters,
>   their nobles with shackles of iron,
> to carry out the sentence written against them—
>   this is the glory of all his faithful people.
> Praise the LORD.

Here we see that the victory of one group over the other is understood to manifest the glory of God. To translate this into the Roman situation is to understand one reason why the house churches were so hostile to one another. They each apparently believed, as a broad stream of the biblical tradition did, that triumphing over the other would manifest God's glory. This belief is also the predominant idea of glory in the Islamic tradition and is widely popular in American religious and civic traditions. Probably nothing is more basic for our people than the idea that victory over evil enemies manifests the truth and glory of God. We may understand this today in more secular terms, but the ideas go right back to the Old Testament legacy.

The idea of victory over another is precisely what Paul has reversed in Romans. In place of the triumph of the weak over the strong or vice versa, Paul argues that the manifestation of God's glory comes through mutual respect and interaction. The theme of God's glory, therefore, places the issue of tolerance in a healthy context. To give glory to God is to place humans in their rightful spot as creatures whom it is dangerous to glorify. In this sense the "righteousness of God" that is the theme of Romans comes to its rightful expression only when "God's glory" in its rightful sense is revealed. And this occurs, according to Paul, not when one group triumphs over the other, but when all groups submit to the lordship of Christ.

DIMENSION THREE:
WHAT DOES THE BIBLE MEAN TO ME?

Subjection to the Government

Since Romans 13:1-7 was used in different ways by different people during the time of the American Revolution, it might be interesting to ask the members of your group how they might have placed themselves in relation to Romans 13 during that period. It could be that people would have answered the question differently in 1776 than they are inclined to answer it today. This discussion can help us realize that the appraisal of the relative justice of the government at any one time is crucial for one's understanding of Romans 13.

The Deeds of Darkness

The "deeds of darkness" that Paul mentions at the end of Romans 13 were related to forms of behavior that were highly popular in the Greco-Roman world. An average week of American television (news, drama, and comedy shows) would provide examples of each of these deeds. Bringing some of this material to mind in your lesson might well sharpen the distinction that Paul describes. You need to be careful, however, of falling into a biased assessment of popular entertainment.

Mutual Upbuilding

Romans 14 may help the members of your group distinguish between destructive and helpful criticism. The theme of "mutual edification" in 14:19 is important in this context. This theme implies that each person in the Christian community is responsible for urging others to remain true to their foundations and to grow on their own roots. This implies that the church needs to hold people accountable to their own standards. "Mutual edification" would imply that conservatives and liberals should each seek to encourage the growth of the other, each on the foundations of his or her own faith.

The Issue of Tolerance

In the highly politicized public arena and religious sphere today, both religious and political toleration seem almost impossible. Given that, at the extremes (and perhaps closer to the middle), persons on different sides of the divide easily demonize entire groups without consideration of the complexity of the range of beliefs within the group, how can persons of good faith hope to have meaningful dialogue aimed at mutual understanding? What efforts in your church or community are there to try to bring diverse groups of people together? What sort of preparatory work needs to undergird plans for dialogue, reconciliation, and cooperation?